Top 25 locator map
(continues on inside
back cover)

◄

TwinPack
Costa Blanca

SALLY ROY

Sally Roy is a freelance
Scottish travel writer with a
long-held affection for the
south of Spain, where she has
family ties. She has written and
contributed to numerous
guides on Britain and Europe
including *AA Spiral Spain*, *AA
Spiral Venice*, *AA CityPack
Madrid* and *AA CityPack
Barcelona*.

If you have any comments
or suggestions for this guide
you can contact the editor at
Twinpacks@theAA.com

AA Publishing
Find out more about AA Publishing
and the wide range of travel publications
and services the AA provides by visiting
our website at *www.theAA.com/bookshop*

Contents

About this book

KEY TO SYMBOLS

➕ Grid reference to the Top 25 locator map

✉ Address

☎ Telephone number

🕐 Opening/closing times

🍴 Restaurant or café on premises or nearby

🚉 Nearest railway station

🚌 Nearest bus route

🚢 Nearest riverboat or ferry stop

♿ Facilities for visitors with disabilities

✋ Admission charge

↔ Other nearby places of interest

❓ Other practical information

➤ Indicates the page where you will find a fuller description

ℹ Tourist information

TwinPack Costa Blanca is divided into six sections. It includes:

- The author's view of the Costa Blanca and its people
- Suggested walks and drives
- The top 25 sights to visit
- The best of the rest: what makes the Costa Blanca special
- Detailed listings of restaurants, hotels, shops and nightlife
- Practical information

In addition, easy-to-read side panels provide fascinating extra facts and snippets, highlights of places to visit and invaluable practical advice.

CROSS-REFERENCES
To help you make the most of your visit, cross-references, indicated by ➤, show you where to find additional information about a place or subject.

MAPS
The fold-out map in the wallet at the back of the book is a large-scale map of the Costa Blanca.
The Top 25 locator maps found on the inside front and back covers of the book itself are for quick reference. They show the Top 25 Sights, described on pages 24–48, which are clearly plotted by number (**1**–**25**, not page number) in alphabetical order. The grid references given in this book refer to these maps.

PRICES
Where appropriate, an indication of the cost of an attraction is given:
✋ Expensive, Moderate or Inexpensive.
An indication of the cost of a restaurant is given by € signs: €€€ denotes higher prices, €€ denotes average prices, while € denotes lower prices.

COSTA BLANCA
life

Costa Blanca Life

A Personal View

THE LANGUAGE

Much of the Costa Blanca lies in Valencia, an autonomous province which recognises two official languages, Valencian and Spanish. The dominance of these languages varies from place to place. You may hear either spoken, and will certainly notice both if you are driving. So be prepared for different spellings of the same place and warning signs in either language. Place names in this book are given in Castilian Spanish first, followed by the local Valencian spelling in brackets, where appropriate.

A fisherman repairs his nets in Santa Pola

Fifty years ago the Costa Blanca was an undeveloped coast dotted with fishing villages and backed by peasant farms and barren hills. Today, it is one of Europe's major holiday playgrounds, attracting millions of visitors who flock here year-round to enjoy good-value sun-sand-and-sea holidays.

Most tourists are happy to stay on the coast, where there's everything they need – good hotels, shops and bars, international-style restaurants and entertainment. Second-homers can purchase property in developments where Spanish is never heard, and buy familiar food in foreign-owned shops. Clubs and sports centres are ideal places to make new friends, and everyone speaks English, German or Dutch. Every year the *urbanizaciones* spread inexorably further and further along the coast as the Costa Blanca becomes increasingly a self-contained community, divorced from the real Spain. Few visitors discover the Spanish heart of this beautiful part of the Mediterranean.

This Spanish heart is truly lovely, a land of huge variety, with thriving cities, bustling ports and a booming agricultural industry. Life for Spaniards, thanks largely to tourism, has become immeasurably easier. The people who live here are immensely proud of the region they've seen change out of all recognition in just one generation. Get away from the big resorts, explore the hinterland by car, visit the inland cities where tourism takes second place to everyday life, walk the coastal and country paths and discover for yourself the wonderful diversity of the region. What will stick in your mind is not the international blandness of the coastal strip but the beauty and fertility of the land and the vibrancy of the towns. There are soaring ochre peaks and hidden verdant valleys, almonds and olives, cherries and grapes, figs and oranges. Some stretches of coast are still unspoilt, places where twisting paths lead through aromatic shrubs and pines down to turquoise water. Wading birds forage in shimmering salt flats and birds of prey hover on thermals high above deep canyons. Inland, quietly prosperous towns pursue their traditional ways and villages celebrate their annual fiestas with wholehearted *joie de vivre*. Traditional craftsmanship still flourishes – pottery and basketware, textiles and leatherwork. Every town and village has its own local delicacies and special recipes. There's a whole world waiting to be discovered.

It's this combination of the familiar and the foreign that makes the Costa Blanca so alluring. If you tire of the beaches you can slip into real Spain, and if Spain becomes too much, familiar pleasures are waiting back on the coast. At resorts like Benidorm, Alicante, Dénia, Jávea and the towns around the Mar Menor you can pick and choose the best of both worlds, combining the resort pleasures of sun, sea and beach with more typically Spanish pastimes – eating late, strolling home in the balmy air, tracking down some local entertainment. Discovering the dual nature of the Costa Blanca will enhance every aspect of your holiday – and give you memories that will endure long after the tan has faded.

BOUNDARIES

Since Spanish decentralisation and the establishment of the autonomous regions in the 1980s, the Costa Blanca strictly speaking is now only the area within the region of Valencia. The Murcian coast, running from San Pedro del Pinatar to Aguilas, is officially divided into the Costa Cálida in the north and the Costa del Almería in the south. This book includes Murcia.

The bustling city of Alicante

Costa Blanca in Figures

GEOGRAPHY AND CLIMATE

- The Costa Blanca officially lies along the coastline of the region of Valencia, but this book includes the hinterland and the region of Murcia (► 7, side panel).
- At 325km, the Segura is Spain's eighth longest river.
- Espuña, with a height of 1,579m, is the area's highest mountain.
- There is one regional park and several natural parks, including marine reserves, within the area.
- The northern part of the Costa Blanca enjoys 3,147 hours of sunshine annually, and the southern 3,098 hours.
- The annual rainfall ranges from 148mm to 394mm and occurs mainly in the winter months.

PEOPLE

- The population of the area is more than 2,350,000, most living in the cities and their suburbs.
- Only around 50 per cent of the area's inhabitants were born here of local parents.
- Over 70 per cent of foreign property owners are English or German.

AGRICULTURE AND INDUSTRY

- The main fruit crops are oranges, lemons, cherries, peaches, nectarines and loquats.
- Large amounts of almonds and olives are grown here and are important Spanish exports.
- Local produce includes rice, tomatoes, peppers, courgettes, beans, aubergines and a range of lettuces, which are exported throughout Europe.
- Fruit and nut processing are major industries.
- Shoe manufacture is an important source of revenue.

Bringing in the harvest in the wine town of Monóvar

People of the Costa Blanca

Artists

This part of Spain has given birth to many eminent Spaniards, who have made their mark on local history. World famous are the writer Gabriel Miró Ferrer, who was born in Alicante, and Murcia's most famous son, the 18th-century sculptor Francisco Salzillo. Salzillo specialised in life-size painted wooden figures, which adorn altarpieces and are used in religious processions throughout Murcia.

Nobles

One particularly notable local family of the north, the Borjas of Játiva (Xàtiva), Italianised their name to Borgia when they settled in Rome. A powerful aristocratic family, a branch later moved to Gandía where they built themselves a sumptuous palace. The Roman Borgias flourished, producing two popes, Calixto III and his nephew, Alexander VI, both supreme practitioners of nepotism. Alexander was instrumental in carving up the New World between Spain and Portugal and also fathered a son, the notorious Cesare. This stylish but infamous man, on whom Machiavelli modelled *The Prince*, conspired to have his brother murdered and was involved in constant sexual intrigue and power politics.

Before Tourists

Today, tourism has changed the Costa Blanca forever, and the 19th- and early 20th-century travellers who explored this coastline would scarcely recognise it. One of the last people to write about the area before the boom was Rose Macaulay, who travelled along the coast and described sleepy villages that are now buzzing resorts.

The Rich and Famous

Luxurious villas, hidden in pine woods above the sea, are retreats for European celebrities, business people, sportsmen and women and their families. Many famous people have found the area ideal for a second home, as it allows them to escape media attention.

Below: *the artist José de Ribera (known as El Españoleto) was born in Játiva in 1591*

A Chronology

*c*50,000 BC	First evidence of cave dwellers in painted caves at Villena and Benidoleig.
Pre-1000 BC	The Iberians arrive from North Africa.
*c*1000 BC	Phoenicians establish trading centres. Játiva (Xàtiva) and Elche (Elx) date from this period. The Phoenicians introduce the pottery wheel.
*c*650 BC	Greeks establish trading colonies along the coast and introduce olives, grapes and figs.
500 BC	Carthaginians invade Spain.
218–201 BC	The Second Punic War. Hannibal marches his Carthaginian troops along the Costa Blanca, through France and over the Alps. Rome invades. Latin is introduced.
AD 555	The Roman Empire is collapsing. Visigoths are the dominant power for the next 100 years.
711	Moors invade the Spanish peninsula through Gibraltar and occupy Alicante by 718.
718–1095	Moorish occupation. The Moors introduce irrigation and paper manufacture. They also plant orange, peach and almond orchards and cultivate date palms, rice, sugar cane and cotton.
1095	Moorish Spain becomes a province of the North African Berber empire.
1212	The first decisive Christian victory against the Moors in north Spain launches the Reconquest.
1243	Murcia is conquered by Ferdinand III and becomes part of Castile.
1238–1248	Jaime I of Aragon ousts the Moors from Alicante.
1492	The last Moors are expelled from Granada, along with Spanish Jews.
1519	Revolt against the nobility and the persecution of the *Moriscos* (converted Moors) in Valencia.

1609	The *Moriscos* are expelled.
1701–1714	The War of Spanish Succession between Philip of Anjou and Charles, Duke of Habsburg. Philip's claim to the Spanish throne is ratified by the Treaty of Utrecht.
1808–1812	War of Independence (Peninsular War) against the French. First Spanish constitution is written.
1833–1836	Present provincial boundaries are fixed.
1858–1862	Rail line from Madrid to Murcia/Alicante is built.
1923	Miguel Primo de Rivera becomes dictator.
1931	Alfonso XIII goes into exile.
1936–1939	Spanish Civil War. Alicante and Murcia remain Republican.
1939	General Franco, the leader of the Nationalists, becomes *caudillo* (leader) of Spain.
1960–1970	Tourism booms on the Costa Blanca.
1975	Franco dies; Juan Carlos becomes king.
1982	Valencia (including Alicante) and Murcia are established by statute as autonomous regions.
1986	Spain becomes part of the European Community, with the fastest-growing economy in western Europe.
Early 1990s	Spain suffers a recession.
1999	The Partido Popular party wins again in Valencia and Murcia in regional government elections.
2002	Euro notes and coins are introduced, replacing the Spanish peseta.
2004	After the horrific act of terror in Madrid, José Luis Zapatero (PSOE) replaces José María (PP) Aznar as president-elect.

Best of the Costa Blanca

Taking a break for refreshments in Calle Trapería, one of Murcia's smartest shopping streets

Above: *strings of lights decorate the promenade in Benidorm*
Below: *you can't visit coastal Spain without trying a traditional paella*

If you have only a short time to visit the Costa Blanca, or would like to get a complete picture of the region, make time for at least some of these essentials:

- Relax on a sandy beach or enjoy a cooling swim off one of the rocky headlands on the northern coast.
- For lunch, fill up on a selection of tapas, delicious bar snacks ranging from fresh seafood, *tortilla* and olives to dried ham, crumbly *Manchego* cheese and salted almonds.
- Take the scenic Costa Blanca Express between Alicante and Dénia for great views and glimpses of small-town life. Or hop on at night and have dinner up the coast from your resort.
- For fresh breezes and a change of scene, take a boat ride to Tabarca, Benidorm Island or the islands in the Mar Menor.
- Go to a local market and admire the produce, smell the flowers and buy a picnic, a paella pan or a pair of locally made sandals.
- Explore inland from the coast and discover hilltop villages, lush market gardens, historic towns and splendid mountain landscapes.
- Pass an evening Spanish-style: take a stroll along a palm-lined boulevard, have a leisurely drink, do a little late shopping, have dinner at 10:30, then listen to some live music.
- Have a gastronomic day out sampling local wine, traditional paella and *turrón*, a delicious almond-based confection produced here to be eaten at Christmas.
- Take in a fiesta, be it the pre-Lent *Carnaval*, the Holy Week processions, a *Moros y Cristianos* parade commemorating the Reconquest or a summer firework display.
- Tuck into a Benidorm English breakfast with real tea and all the trimmings.

COSTA BLANCA
how to organise your time

A Walk Around Alicante

Start at the east end of the tree-lined, tessellated Explanada de España and cut north for two blocks into the Plaza del Ayuntamiento, to emerge opposite the town hall (► 24), with its marvellous façade and twin towers. Turn right along the Calle de Jorge Juan then left up the steps to the Plaza de Santa María. The lovely Gothic church (► 56) is finely balanced by the Museo de la Asegurada (► 24).

INFORMATION

Distance 2km
Time 2–3 hours, depending on visits
Start/end point Explanada de España
▣ S, G, M
Lunch Darsena (€€)
✉ Muelle de Levante 6, Marina Deportiva
☎ 965 20 75 89

Take the steps up the narrow Calle Instituto, by the museum, and turn left into the Plaza del Puente, the site of the Pozos de Garrigos underground water tanks. Follow the Calle de Toledo left out of the plaza until you reach the Plaza del Carmen. This is the heart of the Barrio Santa Cruz, the oldest part of Alicante.

Cross the square and take Carrer San Rafael, right, up some steps. Near the top turn left into Carrer de San Antoni, then right up Calle Dipurado Auset (sign to Ermita de Santa Cruz) up more steps. Here is the Ermita de Santa Cruz, a 19th-century shrine lying just below the Torreón de la Ampollo, one of old wall's surviving towers.

Walk back along San Antoni and turn right down the steps, then left down San Rafael to return to Plaza del Carmen. Cross the square and continue down Carrer de Argensola to Plaza de San Cristóbal, where you turn left down Calle Labradores, lined with 18th-century houses and leading to San Nicolás cathedral (► 56). Head west along the Calle de Miguel Soler to Rambla de Méndez Núñez, where you turn left towards the sea. A left turn at the bottom brings you back to the Explanada de España.

The Explanada de España is a favourite spot for relaxing in the shade

A Walk Around Benidorm

Start at the seafront at the corner of Avenida d'Alcoi and Avenida Martínez Alejos and walk inland for 100m. Turn left into old Benidorm, a fishing village until the 1960s, along Gats Ricardo, and go up the steps of the delightful Carrer dels Gats to Plaça del Castell.

This pretty clifftop square, dominated by the blue-domed church of San Jaime, gives wonderful views of the whole stretch of Benidorm Bay, with Playa de Levante (► 51) to the north and Playa de Poniente to the south. The dramatic promontory beyond Poniente is the Sierra Helada (Serra Gelada, ► 47).

Turn south to the Plaça de la Senyoria, take the flight of steps, left, down to the jetty, turn right along Passeig de Colon and right again along Passeig de la Carretera, the old town's main street.

Look out on your left for the entrance to the covered Mercado Municipal, packed with fascinating fish and meat stalls and a good place to buy a picnic. Turn left onto Calle Tomás Ortuño (not marked on the turning), narrow here, but widening as it runs uphill towards the new part of town, and full of food and household shops.

Take a right turn down Calle Escoles and cross the junction to Calle Hondo. A short flight of steps leads down to the Parque de L'Aigüera (► 52), a haven of green and soothing fountains. Walk up through the park to the top left-hand gate. From here Benidorm's impressive Plaza de Toros can be seen above. Cross the Avenida de L'Aigüera and go through Calle San Marco to rejoin Tomás Ortuño.

INFORMATION

Distance 2.5km
Time 1.5–2 hours
Start point Avenida d'Alcoi
🚍 3, 12
End point West end of Calle Tomás Ortuño
🚍 6
Lunch Pulpo Pirata (€)
✉ Calle Tomás Ortuña
☎ 966 80 32 19

A pot of red geraniums sits beneath a traditional ceramic sign in Benidorm

15

A Drive to the Sierra de Aitana

Take the E15 motorway north from Alicante and exit onto the C3318 (70) running inland to Callosa de Ensarriá. Continue on this road to visit the Fuentes del Algar (➤ 60). Cut back to Callosa and take the C3313 (755) into the hills, towards Guadalest.

As the road climbs, terraces first levelled in Moorish times and washed with the pink of almond blossom in February cling to the lower slopes. The road rises steadily until a sharp corner brings Guadalest (➤ 33) into view.

After visiting the village and its castle, continue upwards past the white villages of Benimantell and Confrides to cross the pass of Puerto de Ares.

The village of Benimantell

As you lose height, the vegetation changes and pines and olives dot the terraces and hillside. Through Ares village turn left onto the A170 and past Alcolecha.

The superb landscape of the Sierra de Aitana is scattered with pines, juniper, herbs and aromatic shrubs. After 9km take the left fork onto the A173 to Sella, passing the Safari Aitana (➤ 59).

The upland scenery, with the ochre-coloured peak of Aitana (1,558m) surging up from the valley, gives way gradually to impeccably kept terracing once more. Orange and almond trees are underplanted with vegetables and salad plants. Drive through Sella and after 6km take a left turn onto the A1741 to Finestrat, and then the A1735 to return to Benidorm, Alicante and the coast.

A Drive from Pego to La Nucia

Start at the lively town of Pego. Once surrounded by rice fields, it feels a long way from the coastal resorts. It still retains its wide town gates and the parish church has a lovely 15th-century altarpiece of the pregnant Madonna.

Leave the town by the C3318 (715) heading southeast to Orba. After Orba, follow the road into the hills towards the Coll de Rates pass (➤ 55). As the road climbs superb views open out towards the coast: villages scattered across the plain, a patchwork of fields and ever-widening glimpses of the sea and the coastal massifs. There are several points where you can stop to admire the views.

Once over the pass the scenery becomes, if possible, even more breathtaking as the road descends towards the Guadalest valley and the Fuentes del Algar (➤ 60). Terraces are planted with almonds, loquats and oranges and the dramatic crags of Aixorta rise up to the south.

Continue on the C3318 (715) all the way to Polop, an everyday inland town in the foothills. Lovely old buildings line the narrow streets and there is a church, ruined castle and a clutch of good restaurants. The town's main attraction is the Font Els Xorros, an ancient fountain with 221 spouts.

Continue on to La Nucia, which hosts a large and popular street market on Sundays.

INFORMATION

Distance 55km
Time 2 hours without stops, all day with visits and shopping
Start point Pego
✚ E1
End point La Nucia
✚ E2
Lunch Ca L'Angeles (€€)
✉ Gabriel Miró 16, Polop
☎ 965 87 02 26

Some of Pego's rich stone architecture

A Drive into the Sierra de Espuña

INFORMATION

Distance 120km
Time 4.5 hours without stops, or a full day with visits
Start/end point Alcantarilla
🚆 A3
Lunch Venta La Magdalena (€)
✉ Baños de Mula
☎ 968 66 05 68

Head northwest out of Alcantarilla on the C415, exit 651 from the Vía del Mediterráneo (E15).

You soon leave behind the light industry and built-up areas to drive through some of Murcia's fertile *huerta* (gardens), with acres of orange, almond and peach trees. As the road rises the vegetation thins and the mountains dramatically rise up to the west. At Mula (► 40) turn left off the bypass onto the C3315 to Pliego.

Pliego is a historic town lying on one of the old transhumance routes. These ancient tracks, used until comparatively recently by shepherds to move stock from summer to winter pastures, criss-cross many Mediterranean regions.

After Pliego the road climbs steadily towards the village of Gevar. Once through the village look out after 6km for a right turning onto an unclassified road signposted Albergue Juvenil 8.5km.

This is the start of the route that climbs through the Sierra de Espuña (► 46), one of Spain's larger regional parks. This tortuous mountain road traverses the park through breathtaking mountain scenery, with wonderful viewpoints and good picnic places.

The road eventually drops down to join the MU503 at Aledo (► 46). Follow this to Totana (► 76). Then take the E15 motorway back to your start point at Alcantarilla.

This unusual statue enjoys excellent views over the Sierra de Espuña

A Drive from Dénia to Benissa

Take the AP132 east from Dénia through the fringes of the Montgó natural park (▶ 39). After 6.5km turn left on to Carretera el Cap de Sant Antoni.

This road runs through an unspoilt tract of pines and scrub to the Cabo de San Antonio (▶ 39), with its lighthouse and superb views.

Backtrack to the main road and turn left to visit Jávea (Xàbia, ▶ 38). Head south past the beaches and take the A1334 to Cabo de la Nao (▶ 55), branching left onto the AP1331, which runs out to the point.

The road runs through pine woods dotted with enviable villas and tracks leading down to hidden beaches. It's worth making the detour to Playa de la Barraca (▶ 50) before continuing to the cape, with another lighthouse and a wonderful cliff vista.

Retrace your route up from the beach and after 2km turn left onto the AV1332 to the sheltered cove of La Granadella (▶ 50). Drive almost back to Jávea then turn left and left again, following signs to Benitatxell on an unclassified road running through vineyards. At the T-junction turn left onto the AV1341 to Benitatxell, a laid-back village. Continue on the AV1341 through Teulada, then take the N332 (which is signposted C332) to Benissa, with its historic Old Town.

INFORMATION

Distance 65km
Time 2.5 hours or all day with stops for sightseeing
Start point Dénia
⊞ F1
End point Benissa
⊞ F2
Lunch Bar-Restaurante Cabo La Nao (€€)
✉ Faro Cabo La Nao
☎ 965 77 18 35

One of Jávea's winding streets

Finding Peace & Quiet

MOUNTAIN WALKING

Walking in the sierras is becoming increasingly popular, and there are good publications and tourist office leaflets available to guide you. Remember to let someone know where you are going and when you expect to be back, wear suitable clothes and footwear, be prepared for the weather to change and take plenty of water and something to eat. Detailed maps are available from the Centro Nacional de Informacíon Geográfica, General Ibáñez de Ibero 3, 28003 Madrid (☎ 915 97 95 14; www.cnig.es). Local tourist boards can put you in touch with walking groups.

Walking in dappled shade in the Sierra de Aitana

As in so many parts of Spain, tourism in the Costa Blanca clings to the highly developed coastal strip, leaving the hinterland virtually untouched. Less than 8km inland from even the busiest resort, Spanish rural life continues as it has always done. So if you crave tranquillity you never have far to go, with the added bonus that this lovely coast is backed by some wonderful countryside.

THE COAST

Even beside the sea there are still undeveloped pockets where you can have a swim or a clifftop walk far from the sights and sounds of the 21st century. There are some impressive pine-studded cliffs and solitary coves south of Cabo de la Nao (Cap de la Nau, ► 55), stretches of dune-backed secluded sand between Alicante and Torrevieja, and remote, empty bays and beaches at Calblanque (► 27) below Cabo de Palos, now a designated natural park. These coastal areas have an exceptionally rich spring flora. Lavender, thyme, rosemary, white, yellow and pink cistus and other aromatic plants carpet the cliffs from March to June. Some parts of the coastal water have remarkable marine life, which flourishes on the expanses of sea grass, and includes the now-rare turtle. The salt flats around Santa Pola and Torrevieja provide rich feeding for more than 250 species of birds, including some bee-eaters and flamingo colonies.

THE HINTERLAND

South of Alicante the area behind the coast-line is relatively flat and very fertile, planted with vegetable crops and huge orange groves, the landscape dotted with small farms and sentinel palm trees. The palms form a forest around Elche (Elx, ► 30), where you can stroll in shady peace. South again, Murcia seems like one vast market garden, the upper Segura Valley a rolling landscape of peach orchards, olive groves and rice fields interspersed with patches of woodland, steep escarpments and sleepy country towns. The vibrant colours of poppies, sunflowers and

Bermuda buttercups border its quiet roads. This agricultural landscape provides shelter for a good range of birds and small mammals. Naturalists keen on insects and small reptiles will find fascinating life in the stone walls and long grasses bordering the well-tended fields.

Cycling is one way to enjoy the extensive views across the Sierra de Espuña

THE MOUNTAINS

North of Benidorm the high sierras rise precipitously from the coast; wonderful mountain systems of great drama, the bare rockfaces glow with different colours as the light changes throughout the day. The lower slopes of these great mountain valleys have been intricately terraced since Moorish times and are planted, as they have been for centuries, with almonds, oranges, loquats, cherries and olives. Roads twist up through the mountains, sometimes clinging to the hillsides, sometimes allowing stupendous panoramas of valleys and further chains of peaks and rockfaces. These hills are laced with ancient footpaths offering day-long hikes magnificent for discovering the wildlife, birds and flora. Foxes, rabbits and other mammals are hard to spot in daylight, but the soaring birds of prey, migrant wintering songbirds and prolific insect life add an extra dimension to walking in this superb landscape.

In the south of the region lies another great mountain area, the Sierra de Espuña (➤ 46), a superb mountain chain covered with natural pine woods.

Orange groves flourish in this part of Spain

21

What's On

JANUARY

Los Reyes Magos: parades celebrate the arrival of the Three Kings, all over the Costa Blanca.

Porrate de San Antón (Alicante, Benidorm): a countryside festival with parades, horse-drawn carts, food and a blessing of farm animals.

FEBRUARY

Carnaval: parades and dancing in fancy dress.

MARCH/APRIL

Semana Santa: Holy Week celebrations are particularly noteworthy in Cartagena, Jumilla, Murcia, Moratalla, Orihuela, Alicante and Elche.

Peregrina de Santa Faz: 100,000-strong pilgrimage to the monastery at Santa Faz, Alicante.

Fiesta de la Primavera (Murcia): parades and fireworks in the week following Holy Week. It includes the *Bando de la Huerta* (Orchard Procession) and the *Entierra de la Sardina* (Burial of the Sardine).

Fallas de San José (Dénia): fire-festival with effigies burnt on pyres.

Moros y Cristianos (Alcoy): the most important of the many festivals held to celebrate the Reconquest.

Semana Mediterránea de la Música: international classical performers come to Alicante.

JUNE

Hogueras de San Juan (Alicante): a week-long midsummer festival with parades, fireworks and bullfights. Smaller *hogueras* in Dénia, Calpe (Calp), Benidorm and Jávea (Xàbia).

JULY

Festival Español de la Canción (Benidorm): major Spanish song festival.

Moros y Cristianos (Villajoyosa): spectacular historical mock-battle on the beach.

Fiesta de la Virgen del Carmen (Villajoyosa, Tabarca, San Pedro): processions, boat races, fireworks.

AUGUST

Festival de las Habaneras (Torrevieja): festival of the Cuban songs brought back by salt-exporters.

Misteri d'Elx, La Festa (Elche): medieval mystery play celebrating the Assumption of the Virgin.

Moros y Cristianos (Dénia, Jávea): historical festival.

Fiesta de la Vendimia (Jumilla): a fountain runs with wine to celebrate the wine harvest.

Festival Nacional del Canta de las Minas (La Unión): one of the Spain's key flamenco events.

SEPTEMBER

Festival de Folklore del Mediterráneo (Murcia): international festival.

OCTOBER–DECEMBER

Small local festivals, listed under town entries.

COSTA BLANCA's
top 25 sights

The sights are shown on the maps on the inside front cover and inside back cover, numbered **1** – **25** alphabetically

Alicante (Alacant)

INFORMATION

⊞ D2

ℹ Rambla Méndez Núñez 23
965 20 00 00; www.
comunidadvalenciano.com

❓ *Hogueras de San Juan*
(20–29 Jun); for
additional festivals ➤ 22,
or phone the tourist office

Ayuntamiento (Town Hall)

✉ Plaza del Ayuntamiento 1
☎ 965 14 91 00
🕐 Mon–Fri 8–1
🚌 G, H, M
♿ Good
🎫 Free

The Centre

🍴 Choice of restaurants and
bars (€–€€€)
🚌 F, G, H, K, L, M

Museo de la Asegurada

✉ Plaza de Santa María 3
☎ 965 14 09 59
🕐 Summer Tue–Sat 10–2,
4–9, Sun and hols
10:30–2:30; winter
Tue–Sat 10–2, 4–8
♿ Good
🎫 Free

Curving round a bay and dominated by the ruins of its ancient castle, Alicante remains a truly Spanish city. This is despite its thousands of tourists.

Alicante has everything you would expect of a Mediterranean city: a long and honourable history, venerable buildings, palm-lined avenues, seafront *paseos* and all the amenities of a thriving modern provincial centre. The year-round mildness of the climate, sandy beaches and good hotels are added attractions. It is the second largest city in the Valencia region and the capital of Alicante province, the fourth wealthiest province in Spain. Its prosperity is based on industry, agriculture and tourism.

Alicante's centre consists of the old *barrios*, clustered at the foot of Monte Benecantil, and the broad avenues of the 19th-century city. Head for the Santa Cruz district to find some of the city's oldest buildings, such as the Museo de la Asegurada (a museum of 20th-century art), two 19th-century sanctuaries and great tapas bars.

The twin-towered 18th-century Town Hall (Ayuntamiento) is one of Alicante's finest baroque buildings. The Salón Azul contains the city's earliest charter of privileges and a small picture gallery. The chapel is adorned with beautiful painted tiles, and over the altar hangs a painting of St Nicolás of Bari, the city's patron.

Ramblas Méndez Núñez demarcates the 19th-century commercial centre, home to the colourful Mercado Central. The main shopping area runs along Avenida de Maisonnave and the streets around Avenida de Francisco Soto. This leads down to Paseo de la Explanada de España, a lovely 19th-century palm-shaded walkway running parallel to the sea. Behind the Explanada lie the port and marina, an area well-served by bars and cafes.

Top: *strolling along the Explanada de España*

Alicante's Castillo de Santa Bárbara

This should be the first stop on a tour of Alicante and is a perfect way to get your bearings, while admiring amazing views of the town and coastline.

The rambling complex of fortifications known as the Castillo de Santa Bárbara dominates Alicante from its position on the summit of Monte Benecantil. Rising dramatically on a bare rock above the town, the castle is best viewed from the oldest quarter of Alicante, the *villa vieja*, in the Barrio de Santa Cruz.

The site has certainly been fortified since prehistoric Iberian times and the Carthaginians, Romans and Moors all built here from the 3rd century BC. No traces of their work remain and today's structures date mainly from the 16th century. The castle was repeatedly attacked but proved impregnable until the War of the Spanish Succession. Assaulted from the sea in 1706 by Sir John Leake, it fell to Philip V's French troops in 1708, and was blown up by them in 1709, killing the English garrison. Undeterred, the English returned a century later and occupied the castle throughout the Peninsular War.

Today, the main attraction is the superb view from the top, a vast panorama over the town, from the palm-flanked Explanada through the 19th-century streets and shady plazas to the old quarter, and up and

down the coast with its curving white beaches, headlands, port and marina. You can walk, drive up or take a lift from the Playa del Postiguet that ascends through a shaft cut into the hill.

INFORMATION

➕ D2

✉ Above Playa del Postiguet, Alicante

☎ 965 16 21 28

🕐 Apr–Sep 10–8, Oct–Mar 9–7. Lift operates at same times

🍽 None on site

🚌 G, S

ℹ Alicante: Rambla Méndez Núñez 23 ☎ 965 20 00 00; www.comunidadvalenciano .com

♿ Good

💷 Castle free; lift moderate

↔ Catedral de San Nicolás de Bari (► 56), Ayuntamiento (► 24), Museo de la Asegurada (► 24)

There are glorious views from the Castillo de Santa Bárbara

Altea

🚹 E2

✉ 12km north of Benidorm

🍴 Restaurants/bars
(€–€€€)

🚌 From Benidorm

🚆 From Benidorm

ℹ Calle San Pedro 9 ☎ 965
84 41 14

🎉 *Fogueras de Sant Joan*
(24 Jun), *San Pedro*
(Jul/Aug), *Moros y
Cristianos* (last week
of Sep)

↔ Benidorm (➤ 52), Calpe
(➤ 52)

**Sheltered by steep hills, the town of
Altea tumbles down the slopes
towards the sea. The blue-domed
church of La Virgen de la Consuelo sits
at the top like a cherry on a cake.**

Originally a fishing village, Altea attracted
outsiders right at the start of the development of
the Costa Blanca. The charm of the town,
and the quality of the light, pulled in painters,
craftsmen and potters who, back in the 1950s,
set up an artists' colony in the whitewashed
houses that line the steep lanes. They're still
here, and their presence has indubitably kept
the place from the worst of tasteless development. There may be a plethora of gift and
souvenir shops, but there's also a
great sense of style. Tempting
boutiques line the narrow streets,
while café tables, shaded by orange
trees, spill out onto every open
space. White walls are splashed
with brilliant geraniums, plumbago
and bougainvillaea, and the town's
popularity with tourists ensures
there's a constant babble of voices
in a multitude of languages.

Summer sees the *Muestra de
Artesanía de Altea*, a craft fair
showcasing the best of local work.
You can walk down from the old
town to Altea's beach area, where
there's the usual cluster of
restaurants, hotels and bars ranged
along a pleasant palm-lined
esplanade, and good watersports facilities.

Altea dates back to Roman times and is a real
Costa Blanca gem. But its charms, and its
proximity to Benidorm, inevitably attract huge
numbers of visitors. Come early, or straight after
siesta, to see it at its best.

Top: *the church of La
Virgen de La Consuelo
watches over Altea*
Above: *one of the town's
attractive narrow streets*

Calblanque

Calblanque is a remote and untouched stretch of coast, its secluded bays enriched with flowers, birds and solitude. If you are seeking an unspoilt beach, look no further.

A few kilometres south of the highly developed resorts around the Mar Menor lies one of Spain's most unspoilt coastal stretches, Calblanque. Local people fought hard in the 1980s to protect this area, which is now a designated natural park.

Access is down a bumpy track off the busy main road running to La Manga. Within minutes, the roar of traffic disappears, hills rise up and the road gradually winds down to the sea. From the small car park boardwalks lead across the fragile dunes to the beaches, and paths run along the coast in either direction.

The fine sands and crystal-clear water are only part of the experience, and it's worth leaving the beach to walk along the coast or explore the inland hills. A track runs south towards Cabo Negrete and the lighthouse at Punta Negra. Follow it down to see impressive rock formations caused by water erosion, lovely views and tempting swimming coves. The waters here are wonderfully clear and limpid, with protected underwater vegetation and sea creatures – perfect for scuba divers and snorkellers.

A scramble in the hills behind the coast will give you an idea of the incredible richness of Calblanque's flora and fauna. Apart from other walkers, you may meet a herdsman and his goats, which graze on the aromatic plants.

Calblanque's main attraction is its peace, and its survival as an unspoilt enclave is a good example of what determined public opinion can achieve.

INFORMATION

- B4
- 70km east of Murcia
- Bar occasionally open in summer (€)
- Bus from Cartagena or La Unión to La Manga, then 30- to 50-minute walk
- Small information office in park. Irregular opening hours ☎ 902 11 37 92
- None
- Cartagena (► 57), Mar Menor, La Manga and Cabo de Palos (► 53)

Top: *the rocky shoreline of Calblanque*

27

Cocentaina

INFORMATION

🔲 D1
✉ 60km west of Benidorm
🍴 Choice of restaurants and bars (€–€€€)
🚌 From Alicante
ℹ Palau Comptal, Plaza del Pla s/n ☎ 965 59 01 59
🎉 *Moros y Cristianos* (8–11 Aug); *Fira de Tots Sants* (1 Nov)

Palau Comtal
☎ 965 59 08 69
🕐 Mon–Sat 11–7
♿ Few
💶 Inexpensive

Top: *the recently restored Palau Comtal*
Below: *a watchtower once guarded the town*

Packed with fine old buildings and churches, the thriving inland town of Cocentaina is known for its fiestas and superb local cooking.

Cocentaina is one of the most historic towns in the area and benefits from a prosperous textile industry. It sits in the Serpis Valley, backed by the Sierra de Mariola.

The Christian and Moorish quarters, known as the Vila and the Raval, are still clearly delineated below the ancient castle. The Vila is a medieval maze of streets centring around the Plaça del Pla. Here you'll find the Palau Comtal, a magnificent and recently restored 13th- to 15th-century fortified palace, now the seat of Cocentaina's university. You can visit its lovely rooms, which include the Sala Dorada and the Sala de Embajadores, with tiled Renaissance floors and exuberant baroque ceilings. The chapel of San Antonio and the courtyards are other highlights.

Next to the Palau are two ornate baroque religious foundations, the convent of the Clarisas and the Monastery of the Mother of God. From here, follow the Calle Mayor to visit Cocentaina's main museums. The Museu del Centre d'Estudis Contestans features the story of Cocentaina with displays and an audio-visual programme. The Casa Museu del Fester is devoted to the *Moros y Cristianos* festival.

You could fortify yourself with some tapas – the town specialities include maize *tostons* and meat in spicy sauce – before heading uphill to the 15th-century Gothic castle. Recently restored, it's the town's symbol, with astounding views.

Dénia

Lying beneath the heights of the Montgó natural park, historic, elegant Dénia is a far less brash holiday resort than some of its neighbours.

Inhabited by the Phoenicians and the Greeks, Dénia was named in honour of the Roman goddess Diana. The inhabitants are still known as *dianenses*. English raisin-dealers lived here throughout the 19th century and many are buried in the almost-forgotten English cemetery. The town's broad streets and solid buildings date from this time.

A small Museo Etnológico has displays on the town's early history. Dénia's other attractions include the Castillo de Dénia (castle), perched high above the town and housing a small Museo Arqueológico (archaeological museum), the lovely 18th-century Church of the Assumption and a picturesque old quarter near the fishing port. From here, ferries run to the Balearic Islands and a narrow-gauge train runs down the coast to Alicante (Alacant). But a car is probably the best way to see the lovely coastline to the south.

Dénia has two contrasting beaches. If you like swimming off rocks in clear water, Les Rotes fits the bill and good swimmers can follow the cliffs to the south. La Marineta is a long stretch of safe, clean, sandy beach backed by a tiled esplanade, excellent for children. There are good facilities.

INFORMATION

➕ F1
✉ 55km north of Benidorm
🍴 Choice of restaurants and bars (€–€€€)
🚌 From Benidorm
🚢 To Ibiza and Mallorca: Balearia Lines, Estación Marítima ☎ 902 16 01 80; www.balearia.com
ℹ Oculista Buigues 9 ☎ 966 42 23 67; www.denia.net
❓ *Fallas de San José* (16–19 Mar); *Romería a la Virgen de Rocío* (Jun); *Hogueras de San Juan* (20–24 Jun); *Fiesta de la Santísima Sangre* (2nd Wed after 28 Jun); *Moros y Cristianos y San Roque* (14–16 Aug)
↔ Jávea (► 38)

Below: *colourful buildings in historic Dénia*

Elche (Elx)

Spain's shoe-manufacturing capital is a stronghold of the Valencian language and one of the most historic towns in the region. It is surrounded by Europe's largest palm forest.

INFORMATION

- 🔲 C3
- ✉ 23km southwest of Alicante
- 🍽 Restaurants and bars
- 🚌 From Alicante
- 🚆 From Alicante
- ℹ Parque Municipal
  ☎ 965 45 27 47
- ❓ Elche is known for its festivals, including: *Semana Santa* (Mar/Apr); *Moros y Cristianos* (1–8 Aug); *Misteri d'Elx, La Festa* (11–15 Aug); *Vínguda de la Mare de Déu* (28–29 Dec)
- ↔ Huerto del Cura (► 31), Guardamar del Segura (► 52), Orihuela (► 43), Santa Pola (► 51)

Museu Municipal de la Festa
- ☎ 965 45 34 64
- 🕐 Tue–Sat 10–1:15, 4:30–8:30 (Jul–Aug 5–9), Sun 10–1
- ♿ Excellent 💶 Moderate

Museo Arqueológico Altamira
- ☎ 965 45 36 03
- 🕐 Tue–Sat 10–1, 4–7, Sun 10–1
- ♿ Good 💶 Inexpensive

Convento de la Mercé
- 🕐 Tue–Sat 10–1, 4:30–8:30, Sun 10–1
- ♿ Good 💶 Free

Top: *Elche has some fine Moorish architecture*

Elche began life as an Iberian settlement and was a Phoenician trading centre from *c*1000 BC. The Romans called the town Iulia Illice Augusta, and it went on to become a Visigothic episcopal centre, then a Moorish power base. It was retaken by Jaime I in 1265 and has since quietly prospered.

The old town, on the east bank of the Vinalopó river, contains almost everything worth seeing, although some of the shoe factory outlets in the modern town are worth visiting. The main sights are clustered around the vast baroque basilica of Santa María, whose blue-tiled dome dominates the ancient town centre. Built in the 16th and 17th centuries, the basilica, dark and cavernous inside and a mass of exuberant carving outside, is the scene in August of the *Misteri d'Elx*. You can learn more about this medieval mystery play, dating from the 1260s, at the Museu Municipal de la Festa.

Near the cathedral, Elche's Museo Arqueológico is housed in the Palacio Altamira. The collection includes Iberian pottery and stone pieces from the more important Museo Monográfico de Alcudia. This stands on the site of Illici, one of Spain's most important Iberian centres, a short distance outside Elche.

The town centre has some fine Moorish remains. The Calaforra, or watchtower, has an extraordinary *mudéjar* hallway, while the 15th-century Renaissance façade of the Convento de la Mercé fronts a cloister and a set of Arab baths.

From the centre of the city a pleasant stroll leads through the old Moorish quarter of Raval to the Franciscan monastery church of San José.

Elche's Huerta del Cura

This fascinating botanical garden, within the great palm forest of Elche, is perfect for shady relaxation after a few hours' sightseeing. Dates grown on its trees are eaten by royalty.

More than 300,000 palms grow in Elche, some in verdant parks and shady squares, others lining streets and gardens. Probably originally planted by the Phoenicians in the 4th century BC, these magnificent trees are still watered by the 10th-century irrigation system built by the Moor Abderraman III and are protected by law. Many trees bear dates, and these are often for sale from street vendors.

Within this vast forest, one of only two palm forests in Europe, some areas have been transformed into gardens and parks, the most famous of which are the Huerto del Cura, or Priest's Grove, and the beautifully manicured municipal park.

Huerto del Cura was laid out in the 19th century. Its palms shelter stands of orange and pomegranate trees, while paths wind past glorious displays of cacti and lilies. Beside a lily pond deep in the garden stands a replica of the bust known as the Dama del Elx, a mysterious and enigmatic Iberian figure dating from 500 BC and discovered in 1897 at the nearby hamlet of La Alcudia. The original is now in the Museo Arqueológico in Madrid.

The most famous tree is the Imperial Palm, a vast and ancient hermaphrodite with seven stems, six male and one date-bearing female, growing from the main trunk. The date crop from specific trees has traditionally been for consumption by famous Spaniards. Two palms regularly supply King Juan Carlos and Queen Sofía with dates.

INFORMATION

- ➕ C3
- ✉ Porta de la Morera, Elche, 25km southwest of Alicante
- ☎ 965 45 19 36
- 🕐 Summer daily 9–8:30; winter daily 9–6
- 🍴 Bar (€)
- 🚻 E
- ℹ Elche: Plaza del Parque 3
  ☎ 965 45 27 47
- ♿ Very good
- 💰 Moderate
- ♿ Elche (➤ 30)
- ❓ A miniature train tours Elche's larger groves, or you can hire a bicycle and follow a mapped route through plantations around the city's edge.

The Dama del Elx sits by a cooling pond

Gallinera Valley

INFORMATION

➕ E1

✉ 50km north of Benidorm

🍴 Choice of restaurants and bars (€–€€€)

🚌 None

ℹ From any of the northern resorts

♿ None

❓ *Moros y Cristianos* festival, Planes, 1st Sun in Oct. Most villages have their annual fiesta during Aug

↔ Alcoy (➤ 57), Cocentaina (➤ 28)

The lovely valley of Gallinera is best seen when the blossom of the almond and cherry trees cloaks the slopes in pink and white.

The dramatic mountains behind the northern Costa Blanca are cut by valleys, some narrow and steep, others broad and gentle. They are all exceptionally fertile, meticulously terraced where needed and irrigated by a system devised by the Moors. These valleys are nicknamed after the main crop: the Gallinera has long been known as the Cherry Valley.

A twisting and scenic road runs inland from Pego the whole way up to the village of Planes, passing through superb landscapes. The land was first settled and cultivated by the Moors and you can still trace their influence in the names and layout of the villages. The *Moriscos*, Christianised Moors, stayed on here after the Reconquest and were only finally expelled in 1609. The terracing on the hillside is often Moorish, and walkers can find the ruins of their drystone houses.

The valley is heavily planted with cherry trees, iridescent green and white in spring, speckled with crimson fruit in summer, and interspersed with orange, almond and olive trees. Towering above are the dramatic escarpments and peaks of the sierras, with seductive little roads twisting up the hillsides.

The main settlement is Planes, a white, quintessentially Spanish village, perched on a hill below a ruined 12th-century castle. A 16th-century aqueduct and a hidden blue swimming hole sit in the valley below.

The other tiny villages like Alcalá, Margarida, Benialfaquí and Benitaya all have their charms. Their traditional way of life is a perfect antidote to the more strident, upbeat attractions of the coastal resorts.

A church nestles in the Gallinera Valley

Guadalest

An excursion inland from Benidorm to this Moorish castle, encircled by mountains, makes an ideal early-evening outing.

The mountains of the Sierra de Aitana rise steeply behind Benidorm's coastline, towering above fertile valleys and dotted with hilltop villages. The land was terraced and irrigated by the Moors, who built a network of castles from which they controlled the northern valleys.

The most dramatically sited of these fortress villages is Guadalest, perched on a rocky crag above terraced orchards and a lake. Its 15th-century castle seems precariously balanced on the summit of the rock. Driving inland from the coast, the best view of the castle is from the almond terraces and olive groves on either side of the twisting road below the village. A few further bends and you reach the castle, surrounded by a maze of narrow streets, whose only access is by a tunnel cut through the rock. Steep slopes drop to the reservoir below, and across the water the mountains, speckled with vegetation and cut by thread-like tracks, soar up over 1,066m.

Jaime I of Aragon seized control of an earlier castle on the site after a lengthy siege in the 13th century. The current castle survived an earthquake in 1644 and successfully repelled Charles, Duke of Habsburg, during the War of the Spanish Succession in the early 18th century. Attractions include small museums and gift shops. Try to visit in the early evening, when the tour buses have left.

INFORMATION

- ⊞ E2
- ✉ 28km northwest of Benidorm
- ☎ 965 88 52 98
- 🕐 Castle: Mar–Oct 10–2, 3–7; Nov–Feb 11–2, 3–7
- 🍴 Bars and restaurants (€–€€€)
- 🚌 From Benidorm
- 🛈 Benidorm: Plaza de Reyes de España ☎ 966 81 54 63; www.benidorm.org
- ♿ Few
- 💶 Moderate
- ↔ Fuentes del Algar (► 60), Guadalest Valley (► 34), Sierra de Aitana (► 45)

Guadalest's Moorish castle clings to the rock

Guadalest Valley

INFORMATION

➕ E2

✉ 15km north of Benidorm

🍴 Choice of restaurants and bars (€–€€€)

🚌 From Benidorm

❓ Fiestas in Benimantell, Beniardá, Benifato and Confrides

🔄 Guadalest (➤ 33)

Most visitors to the Costa Blanca make the trip to the castle at Guadalest, but few explore further into the valley. They're missing out – it's one of the most beautiful in the province.

Blessed by the Guadalest river and abundant springs, the Guadalest Valley was first terraced and irrigated by the Moors, and is sheltered on all sides by high mountains and dramatic peaks. These create a micro-climate ideal for the wide range of fruit trees that have been grown in this fertile zone for centuries.

The oranges and loquats with which the lower slopes are planted give way to almonds as the road climbs. In early spring the entire hillside is a sea of pink blossom. Olive trees gradually appear to replace the almonds, only to be superceded by pine and mountain shrubs as the road reaches its highest point at the Puerto de Ares, from where another valley system opens out towards Alcoy (Alcoi).

An avenue of almond trees in the scenic Guadalest Valley

Among the white villages strung along the valley road are Benifato, Benimantell, Beniardá and Confrides. Stop in these villages to wander the quaint streets, hung with bougainvillaea and geraniums, and absorb the grandeur of the encircling mountains. The ridge looming up across the valley is the Serra de Xorta. Walkers can pick up a track (PR-V-19) at Benairdá and hike across the valley and over the hills to Castell de Castells. Wildlife is relatively plentiful in the valley. Look out for birds of prey wheeling overhead in particular, while the best time for wild flowers is early spring through to May.

Játiva (Xàtiva)

Játiva has an impressive history. It was here that the Iberians minted coins and the Moors introduced paper manufacture to Europe. The town is the birthplace of two popes and the artist El Españoleto.

The best way to get a feel of the town is to walk, following the route marked on the leaflet available at the tourist office. The old quarter, its streets lined with mansions, runs along the side of the hill that overlooks the whole town. A road runs up this hill to the magnificent castle (► 36) and goes past the lovely early church of San Feliu (► 37). It's a tough walk, so the twice-daily tourist train might prove useful. The panoramic views from the top help explain Játiva's strategic importance through the centuries. Back down the hill an avenue of plane trees divides the old centre from the modern town.

The old town has some wonderful buildings, many dating from Játiva's rebuilding after Philip V burnt the town in 1707. Among them is the collegiate church of La Seu, built with Borja (► 9) money in 1596. Opposite stands the Hospital Real, dating from the 15th century. Look out for the Romanesque church of San Francisco, Sant Pere and the house where Borja Pope Alexander II was born. Other mansions include the Palacio del Marqués de Montortal, a 15th-century building with later additions, and the 19th-century Casa de Diego.

The old town's streets are punctuated with little plazas, many filled with the sound of splashing water from the numerous fountains. The simple one in the tiny plaza outside the Palace of Justice is the town's only surviving medieval fountain. On the edge of the old quarter you'll find the Font de las 25 Canelles, a fountain erected in 1794 with 25 spouts.

INFORMATION

- D1
- 110km northwest of Benidorm
- Choice of restaurants and bars (€–€€€)
- From Alicante
- Alameda de Jaume I, 50
- ☎ 962 27 33 46
- The tourist train leaves from outside the tourist office Mon–Sat 12:30, 4:30, Sun 12, 1, 4:30

Top: *the 15th-century Hospital Real*
Above: *elegant houses in Játiva's old town*

Játiva's El Castell

- ✚ D1
- ✉ Carretera Castillo
- ☎ 962 27 42 74
- 🕐 Oct–Apr Tue–Sun 10–6; May–Sep Tue–Sun 10–7
- 🍴 Bar within castle walls (€)
- 🚌 Tourist train from outside tourist office Mon–Sat 12:30, 4:30; Sun 12, 1, 4:30
- ♿ None
- 💶 Moderate
- ❓ Occasional summer concerts – ask at the tourist office

Játiva's castle has its origins in pre-Roman times

This huge fortress, stretching along a ridge, dominates Játiva. It was once considered the most secure castle in the region and still offers bird's-eye views.

El Castell is actually two castles, one pre-Roman and one later. The section known as the Castillo Menor (lower castle) is the older, occupying a site used by the Iberians, Carthaginians and Romans for earlier fortifications. You can still see sections of Roman stonework, though the majority of the surviving towers and walls were built by the Moors.

Enter through the 15th-century Gothic Hannibal Gateway and climb up through another portal to reach a 10th-century tower and the so-called Queen Himilce Tower, named after Hannibal's wife who was said to have given birth to a son here in 218.

The ruins of the Castillo Mayor (upper castle) are much larger. They form a confusing succession of ancient gateways, crumbling courtyards, guardrooms and towers. These stand on the east side of the castle ridge, divided from the Castillo Menor by an open patio. Highlights are the tiny and beautiful Gothic chapel of Santa María, reconstructed in 1431 on an earlier site, and a series of Arabic cisterns and watchtowers.

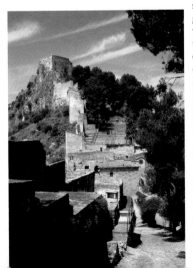

The view from the highest point is well worth the climb. The town lies directly below, with ranges of hills to the south and the ancient frontier with Castille to the east.

Játiva's San Feliu

The evocative and beautiful church of San Feliu is in a lovely position on wooded slopes overlooking Játiva. It dates from the 13th century, making it one of Valencia's oldest churches.

San Feliu (Sant Feliu) is set among olive and cypress trees below the walls of Játiva's historic castle. It is one of the region's finest buildings and is a must for fans of early architecture. The church stands on the site of a 7th-century palaeo-Christian church, the seat of the Visigothic bishopric.

The present building was erected in 1269 on the orders of Jaime I, soon after his expulsion of the Moors. It has a single nave, split by four massive arches, and architecturally is surprisingly similar to Syrian churches of the same date. The church is only rarely used now for services. Its walls are hung with superb Spanish Renaissance religious paintings, mainly from nearby churches and monasteries. Some are sadly in need of restoration, but the colours and gilding still glow. The altarpiece was commissioned at the end of the 15th century and shows scenes from the life of Christ and the Virgin, flanked by images of Saints Cosmas and Damian, two early saints, and Saint Blaise, the patron saint of sore throats. The holy water stoup is carved with scenes from the Nativity, including a shepherd leading two rather charming pig-like sheep. Along the external entrance walls runs a loggia, its roof supported by six Roman columns.

INFORMATION

- ✚ D1
- ✉ Carretera Castillo, Játiva, 60km north of Alicante
- 🕐 Apr–Sep Tue–Sat 10–1, 4–7, Sun 10–1; Oct–Mar Tue–Sat 10–1, 3–6, Sun 10–1
- 🍴 Choice of restaurants and bars nearby (€–€€€)
- 🚃 Tourist train from outside the tourist office Mon–Sat 12:30, 4:30, Sun 12, 1, 4:30
- 🚌 From Alicante via Alcoy
- ℹ️ Alameda de Jaume I, 50 ☎ 962 27 33 46; www.ayto-xativa.org
- ♿ None 🆓 Free

The altarpiece, showing scenes from the life of Christ

Jávea (Xàbia)

INFORMATION

🔖 F2

✉ 55km north of Benidorm

🍴 Choice of restaurants and bars (€–€€€)

🚌 From Benidorm

ℹ Plaza Almirante Bastarreche 11, Aduanas de Mar ☎ 965 79 07 36; Plaza de la Iglesia 6 ☎ 965 79 43 56; www.xabia.org

🎪 *Fogueras de Sant Joan* (24 Jun); *Moros y Cristianos* (last weekend in Jul); *Nuestra Señora de Loreto* (1–8 Sep)

🔄 Dénia (➤ 29), Montgó (➤ 39)

Jávea, believed to be the sunniest place on the coast, is a family-friendly resort with long stretches of beach and a busy working harbour.

Jávea had a long and respectable history before its spread down the hill towards the beautiful and protected beaches. The town lies on a bay embraced by the promontories of Cabo de San Antonio (Cap de Sant Antoni, ➤ 39) to the north and pine-studded Cabo de la Nao (Cap de la Nau, ➤ 55) to the south. The narrow streets of the old town are lined with handsome houses, ornamented with delicate stonework and wrought-iron *rejas* and balconies. Fine buildings cluster around the Plaza de la Iglesia, with its fortified Gothic church of San Bartolomé and dignified town hall.

Just down the street a Gothic palace houses the Museo Arqueológico, Histórico y Etnográfico (archaeological, historical and ethnographic museum). The museum traces Jávea's history from Iberian and Roman times to the emergence of the Christian kingdoms, and gives pride of place to replicas of exquisite Iberian gold jewellery found nearby. The port area, called the Aduanas de Mar, has a busy working harbour. Here you'll find the fish market and fishing boats, the modern church of Nuestra Señora de Loreto with its roof like a ship's hull, long stretches of safe beach and shops, bars and restaurants. Jávea, with its good facilities, friendly atmosphere and easy access to the unspoilt countryside of Montgó (➤ 39), is a popular base for holiday-makers of all ages.

Jávea's bustling harbour

Montgó & Cabo de San Antonio

Montgó is an oasis of unspoilt natural beauty. Visit it, and you'll realise what the Costa Blanca must have looked like before the tourist boom.

The massif of Montgó and the promontory of Planes run down to the Cabo de San Antonio (Cap de Sant Antoni). They are easily reached from Jávea (Xàbia), to the south, and Dénia, to the north. This whole area, covering more than 2,000ha, was designated a natural park in 1987, mainly because of its flora. Within the park more than 600 species of wild flowers grow, many of them unique indigenous sub-species. It is a sheer delight to wander the flower-bordered tracks and paths, breathing air scented with wild rosemary and lavender and murmurous with bees. White, yellow, purple and pink predominate, the low-growing shrubs punctuated by miniature palms, heather, juniper, ilex and pines. The park has much bird life, with some rare gulls along the coast and birds of prey on higher ground.

For serious hikers, there is demanding walking up to the 753m summit, with sweeping views up and down the coast. The less energetic can enjoy several low-level routes. These mainly run through Planes, once heavily cultivated with raisin vines and still scattered with smallholdings. A cypress-lined track takes you to Los Molinos, a line of old windmills above Jávea bay, last used in 1911. The walk (or drive) out to the lighthouse at the cape gives an opportunity for more lovely views and a chance to see the ruins of the tiny 14th-century hermitage dedicated to Saint Anthony, after whom the cape was named.

INFORMATION

➕ F1/2

✉ 40km north of Benidorm

☎ Information centre: 966 42 32 05,

🍴 Choice of restaurants and bars in Jávea and Dénia (€–€€€)

ℹ Jávea: Plaza Almirante Bastarreche 11, Aduanas de Mar ☎ 965 79 07 36; Plaza de la Iglesia 6 ☎ 965 79 43 56; www.xabia.org
Dénia: Oculista Buigues 9 ☎ 966 42 23 67; www.denia.net

♿ None

🔄 Dénia (► 29), Jávea (► 38)

Montgó Natural Park

Mula

🔲 Off map
✉ 32km west of Murcia
🍴 Restaurants and bars
(€–€€)
🚌 From Murcia
ℹ Convento de San
Francisco, Calle Doña
Elvira ☎ 968 66 15 01;
www.mulavirtual.ed
♿ Few
❓ *Semana Santa* (Mar/Apr)
↔ Sierra de España (▶ 46)

Top: *the church of
Santa Domingo*
Below: *the Castillo de
los Veléz*

This town, by the Mula river, is famed for its artisan traditions. Just don't expect peace and quiet if you come during Holy Week!

The narrow streets of Mula's old quarter are truely Moorish in style and are scattered with fine buildings. The old quarter is dominated by the 16th-century Castillo de los Veléz, on the hill behind the town.

Start your explorations at the lovely gardens known as the Glorieta Juan Carlos I, with the adjoining church of San Francisco. Across the park stands the baroque Palacio de Menahermosa, home to a huge collection of Iberian art. Exhibits include weapons, carvings and pottery excavated at a nearby necropolis. From here Calle del Caño climbs steeply up the Plaza del Ayuntamiento. It's worth plunging off to discover the labyrinth of narrow streets on either side. There are more lovely churches around the town. The finest are the 16th-century Santo Domingo, the 17th-century Carmen and the serenely simple 16th-century San Miguel.

The best time to catch Mula is during Holy Week when the town reverberates to the sound of continuous drumming, as the cloaked and hooded figures of hundreds of *tambaradas* patrol the streets. You might also want to visit the nearby reservoir at La Cierva, and the little spa at Baños de Mula.

Murcia

Murcia is a delightful and truly Spanish city that makes few concessions to tourism. Founded by the Moors, it is now a commercial centre.

After its founding in the 9th century, Murcia soon became a key trading centre. Its wealth was based on the fertility of the outlying *huerta* (market gardens). By the 1300s it was the regional capital. Its 18th-century wealth funded the majority of its finest buildings.

Today, it is well worth battling through the modern suburbs to spend time in the historic centre, a largely pedestrianised maze of narrow streets and squares, punctuated by elegant buildings and churches. The major sights, including the cathedral (▶ 42), cluster around the medieval arteries of the Trapería and Platería, today upmarket shopping streets. Here you'll find the bizarre 19th-century Casino, the Teatro Romea, and a clutch of superb churches. Other fine buildings line the river, where there are shady walkways and peaceful green gardens. Murcia's museums include the Museo Arqueológico (archaeological museum) and the Museo Salzillo (Salzillo Museum, ▶ 57). Local pride in traditional artisan work is evident at the Centro Regional de Artesanía, and the city has some excellent restaurants where you can try Murcia's vegetable-based cooking.

The casino, built between 1847 and 1901, is still in use today and was once the town's main social meeting place, offering members a library, meeting rooms, billiard room and ballroom. It is high on a must-see list, and is an eclectic mixture of Moorish features, marble and metalwork, French-inspired grandeur, painted ceilings and English craftsmanship. The high point for most visitors is the ladies' powder room, a neo-baroque fantasy complete with painted ceiling.

INFORMATION

➕ A3
📍 Plaza del Romea 4
☎ 902 10 10 70; Plano de San Francisco s/n
☎ 968 35 87 20;
www.murciaturistica.es
❓ *Semana Santa* (Mar/Apr); Spring Festival (week after Easter); *Entierra de la Sardina* (week after Easter)

Museo Arqueológico
✉ Gran Vía Alfonso X el Sablo 5
☎ 968 23 46 02
🕐 Mon–Fri 9–2, 5–8, Sat 10–2
♿ Good
🎟 Moderate

Centro Regional de Artesanía
✉ Francisco Rabal 8
☎ 968 28 45 85
🕐 Mon–Fri 11–2, 4:30–7:30, Sat 11–2, 5–7

Casino
✉ Calle Trapería 22
☎ 968 21 22 55
🕐 Daily 9:30–9
🍴 Bars and restaurants nearby (€–€€€)
🎟 Free

Top: *Murcia's Glorieta de España*

41

Murcia's Santa María

INFORMATION

➕ A3

✉ Plaza Hernández Amores 2

☎ 968 21 63 44

🕐 10–1, 5–7

🍴 Choice of bars and restaurants nearby

🚌 26, 28, 39, 49

ℹ Plaza del Romea 4
☎ 902 10 10 70;
www.murciaturistica.es

♿ Good

🎟 Cathedral free; museum moderate

🔁 Casino (➤ 41), Museo de Bellas Artes (➤ 57), Museo Salzillo (➤ 57)

Museo de la Catedral

✉ Plaza de la Cruz 2

☎ 968 21 63 44

🕐 Oct–Mar daily 10–1, 5–7;
Apr–Sep daily 10–1, 5–8

♿ Good

🎟 Inexpensive

The façade of this Mediterranean Gothic cathedral is the finest among Murcia's many examples of baroque architecture.

Murcia's cathedral, dating from the 14th to 18th centuries, stands out in a city crammed with exuberant baroque architecture. If ever a building captured the spirit of the place, Santa María, with its ebullient and lavish decoration and sense of religious fervour, surely does.

The cathedral's south side retains its Gothic façade, but the main west front was rebuilt after a flood in 1735. Designed by Jaime Bort, this feast of curves and swooping detail, only slightly restrained by its soaring Corinthian columns, is liberally dotted with statues of gesticulating saints, their robes tossed by some celestial wind.

The interior, retaining signs of its Gothic origin, is an extravagant example of florid plateresque. The high point is the Capilla de los Vélez, completed in 1507 and designed as a funeral chapel for a powerful local family. With its lovely screen and rich vaulting, this must be one of Spain's finest examples of Hispano-Gothic architecture. Other highlights include an urn containing the heart of 13th-century Alfonso the Wise in the Capilla Mayor. The choir contains a *Christ* by Murcia's famous 18th-century resident, Francisco Salzillo. He specialised in realistic polychrome wooden figures to be used in Holy Week processions. His work can be seen at the Museo Salzillo (➤ 57). A ramp and stairway leads up the 98m 18th-century tower, which has great views.

The Museo de la Catedral, in the cloister, houses early sculpture, including a Roman sarcophagus. It gives pride of place to the huge and ornate 600kg gold and silver monstrance, used at the feast of Corpus Christi.

Orihuela

The ancient town of Orihuela makes a good stop if you are seeking a genuine historic inland town, unswamped by tourists.

Orihuela is easily reached from the coast and a visit here could be combined with a trip to Elche (► 30) for a taste of untouched provincial Spain.

Called Aurariola by the Romans, Orihuela stands in the lower reaches of the wonderfully fertile Segura valley, approached through a palm forest. From here, Ferdinand and Isabella embarked on the final push for Granada. Later, the town became a wealthy Renaissance cathedral and university city, the commercial focus for the surrounding area. In the 19th century, a combination of Alicante's new role as regional capital and a destructive earthquake diminished Orihuela's importance. Today the cathedral (► 56), theatre, churches, palaces and historic centre provide a backdrop to everyday life in this prosperous town.

A visit to the Museo Semana Santa will help explain the tremendous impact that Holy Week has in Spain. The museum houses a collection of the massive carved floats, many by Salzillo, used in the processions held during the week before Easter. The ghastly figure known as the Paso de la Diablesa, the She-Devil, and her skeleton companion, have been encouraging sinners to repent since 1688, when Nicolás de Busi created them.

The Seminario de San Miguel stands on the slopes of a hill above the town. It's worth the climb for the tranquillity and good views of the town and fertile plain, and a glimpse of the ruined castle above. Also worth a visit is the Colegio de Santo Domingo, founded as a Dominican monastery and now a private school. Don't miss the refectory, with its stunning *azulejo* frieze.

INFORMATION

- ✛ B3
- ✉ 60km southwest of Alicante
- 🍴 Choice of restaurants and bars
- 🚌 From Alicante
- 🚆 From Alicante
- ℹ Palacio Rubalcava, Francisco Díez 25
  ☎ 965 30 27 47;
  www.aytoorihuela.com
- ❓ *Semana Santa* (Mar/Apr); *Moros y Cristianos* (17 Jul); *Virgen de Monserrat* (8 Sep)
- ↔ Elche (► 30)

Seminario de San Miguel
- ✉ Uphill from Plaza Caturia
- 🕐 Not open to the public

Museo Semana Santa
- ✉ Santa Justa
- 🕐 Mon–Fri 10:30–1:30, 5:30–7:30, Sat 10:30–1:30
- ♿ Good
- 🎟 Free

Colegio de Santo Domingo
- ✉ Calle Miguel Hermandez
- 🕐 Mon–Fri 10:30–1:30, 5:30–7:30, Sat 10:30–1:30
- ♿ Good
- 🎟 Free

Top: *the cathedral at Orihuela*

Peñón de Ifach

INFORMATION

✚ F2

✉ Calpe, 20km northeast of Benidorm

🍴 Bars and restaurants in Calpe (€–€€€)

🚢 Ifach Charter ☎ 965 10 25 91 (summer only)

ℹ Calpe: Avenida de los Ejércitos Españoles ☎ 965 83 69 20, Plaza del Mosquit s/n ☎ 965 83 85 32; www.calpe.es

↔ Calpe (► 52)

Peñón de Ifach is a dramatic headland soaring 330m up from the azure sea and dominating the sandy beaches on either side. Legend claims that Hercules was an early visitor.

No photograph can capture the impact of the huge craggy outcrop, flanked by bustling family beaches, that rears up from the sea at Calpe (Calp). This is the Peñón de Ifach, the symbol of the Costa Blanca, a looming mass of limestone that is geologically related to Gibraltar's rock and is linked to the mainland by a sandy isthmus.

Legend claims that Hercules first charted the Peñón, and the remains of Roman Calpea lie on its slopes. Ifach was certainly used as a watchtower, with warning fires lit on the summit, during the years when the Berber pirates threatened the coast, and it was later renowned as a smugglers' haven.

Today, despite the teeming summer crowds on Calpe's lovely beaches, it remains isolated and untouched, thanks largely to its modern role as a natural park.

A climb to the 332m summit is best tackled in the cool of the morning in the summer. The views along the coastline and inland to the sierras are at their best around sunrise. Allow about an hour to reach the top, along the track which runs through a tunnel in the bottom of the rock face. The gentler lower slopes run down to rocky inlets and tiny bays, and are brilliantly carpeted in spring with a profusion of over 300 species of wild flowers and plants, including an orchid unique to the Peñón.

Bird life is prolific here. In winter the rare Audouin's gull is a frequent visitor and flamingos inhabit the nearby salt flats, along with a variety of waders.

Sierra de Aitana (Serra d'Aitana)

When the coast is sweltering in the summer heat, it's tempting to head for the hills. The Sierra de Aitana is a good choice and is easily accessible from Alicante and Benidorm.

INFORMATION

🏁 D/E2
✉ 30km west of Benidorm
🔄 Guadalest Valley (➤ 34)

The Sierra de Aitana has magnificent scenery… and a safari park!

The Sierra de Aitana offers breathtaking mountain scenery, fresh breezes and cooler temperatures. The range is named after the peak of Aitana, at 1,558m the highest summit in the Costa Blanca's northern sierras. You can drive nearly to the top and there are wonderful views over woodland areas to the surrounding mountains and the coast.

Access is easiest from Sella, an attractive upland town with good facilities and ancient fortifications, or from Alcoleja (Alcolecha), a little further inland.

Children may enjoy a visit to the area's safari park, the Safari Aitana, which also has a swimming pool (➤ 59).

The whole range is marvellous hiking country. A network of paths threads through the hills and over into the Guadalest Valley. You may not have time or energy to walk the whole way, but it's well worth leaving the car and using your own feet. You'll be rewarded with clear air, superb views and the chance to spot birds, trees and wild flowers. It seems a million miles from the bustle of the coast and gives a real taste of the interior.

Sierra de Espuña

INFORMATION

✚ Off map

✉ 25km southwest of Murcia

🍴 Summer-only bar in park, restaurants and bars at Alhama and Aledo (€–€€€)

🚌 From Murcia to Alhama

ℹ Information in summer from the Casa Forestal de Huerta Espuña inside the park. Murcia: Plaza del Romea 4 ☎ 902 10 10 70

🎫 Free

↔ Totana (► 76)

The contrast between the rocky peaks and pine forests of this high sierra and the coast below makes a day in this park an enjoyable change.

Southwest of Murcia city, the Andalucian sierras tail off into a series of rocky massifs. This is the Sierra de Espuña, one of Spain's renowned natural parks, a wilderness area of dramatic peaks and pine forests offering scenic drives, serious climbing and superb walking.

The forest was the inspiration of Ricardo Codorniú, an engineer charged in 1891 with finding a solution to the frequent and destructive floods which swept down from the sierra to the villages below. Huge areas of hillside were planted with Canary pine, cypresses and cedars, which stabilised the slopes and created this unique habitat. Over the last century more than 250 plant species have established themselves, and the forest is home to wild boar, deer, mountain cats and tortoises, as well as more common woodland creatures. At 1,579m, the ochre peak of Espuña dominates the whole park. It is frequently glimpsed through the trees from the road that runs through the park from Alhama to Aledo. This narrow, steep and tortuous road is one of Murcia's most beautiful, and gives access to different areas of Espuña.

Waymarked walking trails run through the woods and tracks give access to challenging rock-climbs. For a more relaxing experience, there are shady glades with natural springs and well laid-out picnic areas.

A lone cyclist travels towards the Espuña peak

Sierra Helada (Serra Gelada)

The 'ice hills' were so-named because of their lower temperatures and the visual effect of the moonlight on the rocky slopes.

Benidorm is sheltered to the north by a mountainous promontory called the Sierra Helada. The whole area is riddled with caves used by the Iberians, and the headland was mined by the Phoenicians and Romans. The coastline was harried throughout the 17th-century by pirate raids and two watchtowers bear witness to its role as a look-out point.

The 21st century has left the Sierra untouched and safe from further development as it is a designated natural park. Few visitors to Benidorm take advantage of this beautiful area, the perfect antidote to the crowded resort. You can take a bus to the north end of the Playa de Levante and strike off into the hills. Tracks lead out to the headlands of Punta de la Escaleta and the lighthouse at Punta Bombarda, while a magnificent path runs along the crest of the ridge, overlooking the sea and coastline. There are precipitous cliffs and seabirds and you can walk for hours without meeting more than a handful of people.

INFORMATION

- E2
- 2km north of Benidorm
- None
- From Benidorm
- Benidorm: Plaza de Reyes de España ☎ 966 81 54 63; www.benidorm.org
- None
- Benidorm (➤ 52)

Top: *the rugged Punta de la Escaleta*
Below: *the Punta Bombarda, with the town of Altea behind*

Tabarca

INFORMATION

☩ C3

✉ 15km south of Alicante

🍴 Restaurants (€€–€€€)

🚢 From Alicante, Cruceros
Kon Tiki ☎ 966 08 21 18;
from Santa Pola, Cruceros
Baeza-Paradi ☎ 965 41
23 38; from Guardamar,
Cruceros Tabarca ☎ 966
70 21 22; from Torrevieja,
Cruceros Tabarca
☎ 966 70 21 22

♿ Few

🔁 Guardamar del Segura
(► 52)

Breezes blow on Tabarca even on the hottest day and the crystal-clear waters tempt snorkellers and divers.

Tabarca is the main island in the Islote de la Cantera archipelago, which lies 15km south of Alicante. Boats run there from several points on the coast, including Alicante, Santa Pola, Guardamar and Torrevieja.

Tabarca was fortified and settled by Carlos III in the 18th century as a prison island for Genoese captives. The mellow old Governor's Mansion now houses an attractive hotel. Much of the original walled town survives, with its stately entrance gate, the Torre de San José, and church of St Peter and Paul. But most summer visitors come here for the beaches, swimming and wonderful fish restaurants. You can escape the crowds by taking an island walk, best in the cool of the evening.

A trip on a glass-bottomed boat is the perfect way to take in some of the incredibly rich marine life that surrounds Tabarca. The waters round the archipelago are a designated marine reserve, with some of the most interesting underwater life along the whole of the Costa Blanca. The shore base is in the old lighthouse, which you can visit on an island walk.

Below: Tabarca's beaches are one of the island's main attractions

COSTA BLANCA's
best

Costa Blanca's Best

Beaches

ÁGUILAS
Well off most foreigners' routes, Águilas is one of the most southerly of the resorts in this area, lying on the Golfo de Mazarrón. This arid stretch of coast is a popular Spanish holiday area that has kept much of its character and escaped the worst type of development. Two excellent beaches and a string of virtually undiscovered coves lie on either side of the town, making it a good base for a tranquil beach holiday.
➕ Off map ✉ 80km southwest of Murcia 🍴 Choice of restaurants and bars (€–€€€) 🚆 From Murcia 🚌 From Murcia ℹ Plaza Antonio Cortijas s/n ☎ 968 48 32 85; www.aguilas.org

ALICANTE'S BEACHES
The Playa del Postiguet, a Blue Flag stretch of beach in the city centre, has excellent facilities and clear water. A short bus ride north, on either side of the Cabo de las Huertas, lie Albufereta and San Juan. Albufereta has good sandy beaches and small rocky coves. San Juan has 7km of sand shelving into the sea, along with hotels, restaurants and sports.
➕ D2 ✉ Alicante 🍴 Bars at all locations (€) 🚌 All served by city buses 🚆 Albuferata and San Juan served by Alicante–Dénia line

LA BARRACA, CABO DE LA NAO (CAP DE LA NAU)
This is a beautiful curved bay, reached down a twisting road past salubrious villas, and sheltered by high pine-clad cliffs and the island of El Descubridor. There is excellent swimming in crystal-clear water off the pebbly beach and plenty of rocks for sunbathing. Reasonable facilities generally available.
➕ F2 ✉ 50km north of Benidorm ♿ Few

CALA SARDINERA, CABO DE SAN MARTÍN (CAP DE SANT MARTÍ)
Unspoilt rocky cove with a pebbly beach sheltered by the cliffs on the north side of Cabo de San Martín. It's a 15-minute hike through rocks and scrub from the nearest parking, followed by a scramble down – worth every step. No facilities.
➕ F2 ✉ 50km north of Benidorm ♿ None

LA GRANADELLA, CABO DE LA NAO
This justly renowned cove is reached by road through pine woods. There's a sickle-shaped bay, where the pale sands and turquoise sea, scattered with boats, are sheltered by soaring pine-covered cliffs. It can be crowded in summer. Reasonable facilities.
➕ F2 ✉ 50km north of Benidorm ♿ Few

Playa de Levante, one of Benidorm's popular beaches

GUARDAMAR DEL SEGURA (► 52)

PLAYA DE BOLNUEVO, PUERTO DE MAZARRÓN
A large area with a variety of beaches and facilities,
Bolnuevo proper has wonderful sand and is sheltered
by sandbars. Opposite here wind and water have
eroded the rocks into fantastic shapes. Hidden coves
lie to the south with superb clear water, ideal for
snorkelling and scuba diving.
🚇 Off map 🖂 70km south of Murcia 🍴 A selection 🐧 Good

PLAYA DE LEVANTE, BENIDORM
Backed by towering hotels, the 2km-long curve of
sand known as the Playa de Levante swarms with
crowds day and night. For most visitors the beach
epitomises Benidorm's attractions – hot sun, clear
blue water, clean white sand. Packed in summer, it
offers wonderful chances to make friends from all
over the world, to show off and to indulge in some
serious people-watching. At night it's transformed
into a brilliantly sparkling chain of lights, the perfect
backdrop for the resort's vibrant night scene.
🚇 E2 🖂 Avenida d'Alcoi/Avenida de Madrid, Benidorm 🍴 Huge
choice of restaurants and bars nearby 🐧 Good

PLAYA DE OLIVA, OLIVA
North of Jávea the coastline is flatter, becoming an
almost continuous strip of sandy beaches, ideal for
small children. The coastal resorts cater efficiently for
large numbers of summer visitors, with hotels,
restaurants, sports facilities, marinas, entertainment
and shops. Playa de Oliva is one of these. Inland lies
the old town, once part of a dukedom founded in 1449
by Alfonso el Magnánimo, with the remnants of the
old ducal castle to be found outside the town. The
surrounding flat, fertile ground, now planted with
oranges, was originally marshland, and some wetlands
remain. The old town centre has some fine 16th-
century buildings and the wonderfully higgledy-
piggledy whitewashed quarter of Santa Ana.
🚇 E1 🖂 42km north of Benidorm 🍴 Choice of restaurants and bars
(€–€€€) 🚹 Passeig Lluís Vivès s/n ☎ 962 85 55 28

PLAYA DEL PEDRUCHO, LA MANGA
The long strip of land separating the Mar Menor from
the Mediterranean is seldom more than a kilometre
across. The warm shallow-water beaches on the inner
side are ideal for children. The windier Mediterranean
water shelves more steeply. The facilities are good.
🚇 B4 🖂 55km east of Murcia 🍴 Restaurants and bars (€–€€€)
🚌 From Murcia 🚍 From Murcia 🐧 Good

PLAYA DE VENECIA, GANDÍA (► 52)

SANTA POLA
Santa Pola is a big, working
port, but south of the town
stretch miles of smooth, clean
sandy beaches backed by
pines and eucalyptus. Behind
these beaches, the salt flats
are a designated natural park,
complete with flamingoes.
🚇 C3 🖂 18km south of
Alicante 🍴 Choice of
restaurants and bars
🚌 From Alicante 🚢 To Isla de
Tabarca 🚹 Plaza Diputación s/n
☎ 966 69 22 76;
www.santapola.es 🐧 Few

51

Coastal Resorts

Palm trees shade the paths of Benidorm's Aigüera Park

Stone steps decorated in the national colours lead through Calpe's Old Town

In the Top 25
🔟 **JÁVEA (XÀBIA, ➤ 38)**
🔢 **DÉNIA (➤ 29)**

BENIDORM

The name Benidorm is synonymous with packed beaches, high-rise hotels and fun. It is a place where four million visitors a year let their hair down and enjoy good-value sunshine holidays. Love it or hate it, you can't criticise the slickness of the operation. Benidorm is justly proud of Aigüera Park, a long sweep of promenades, fountains and greenery running seawards down a dried-up river valley. Its elegant central avenue acts as a meeting place and its two fine amphitheatres are ideal for concerts. Other attractions include the beaches (➤ 50, 51), the charming Plaza de Castillo and the nearby Isla de Benidorm (➤ 60).

➕ E2 🍴 Bars/restaurants (€–€€) ♿ Excellent ℹ️ Plaza de Reyes de España ☎ 966 81 54 63; www.benidorm.org

CALPE (CALP)

The coast north of Benidorm has a chain of good beaches, classy villas hidden behind bougainvillaea-hung walls and relaxed family resorts. Calpe is one of the most popular of these, due mainly to the soaring mass of the Peñón de Ifach (➤ 44). This former fishing village, with its *mudéjar* church, was particularly stalwart during the years of Berber pirate invasion. Its two splendid sandy beaches are often crowded in summer, but you can escape for a boat trip round the Peñón or take a stroll near the salt flats behind town.

➕ E/F2 ✉ 18km north of Benidorm 🍴 Restaurants/bars (€–€€€) 🚌 From Benidorm ⛴ Crucero por la Costa, Explanada del Puerto ☎ 965 85 00 52; Ifach Charter, Explanada del Puerto ☎ 965 84 55 35 ℹ️ Plaza del Mosquit s/n ☎ 965 83 85 32; Avenida de los Ejércitos Españoles 66 ☎ 965 83 69 20; www.calpe.es

GANDÍA

Gandía has more than 20km of clean sand, an elegant promenade and lively restaurants. The star attraction is the sumptuous Palacio de Santo Duque. The town also prides itself on its markets and shops.

➕ E1 ✉ 70km north of Benidorm 🍴 Restaurants and bars (€–€€€) 🚌 From Benidorm ℹ️ Marqués de Campo s/n ☎ 962 87 77 88

GUARDAMAR DEL SEGURA

Surrounded by citrus fruit orchards and vegetable gardens, the ancient settlement of Guardamar is a thriving small town and summer resort. Rolling sand dunes – where you can take a camel ride – make its beaches some of the loveliest on the coast.

➕ C3 ✉ 40km south of Alicante 🍴 Restaurants and bars (€–€€€) ⛴ To Isla de Tabarca, Cruceros Tabarca ☎ 966 70 21 22 ♿ Few

MAR MENOR, LA MANGA AND CABO DE PALOS

The Mar Menor, Murcia's holiday playground, was formed as sand and rocks gradually advanced outwards from two headlands, slowly transforming the original bay into a vast lagoon. The strip of land separating the lagoon from the Mediterranean is called La Manga, 'the sleeve'. Today it's a solid strip of hotels, apartment blocks, shops, restaurants and bars. The landward shore of the Mar saw some development in the 19th century when Spaniards from Murcia built spacious holiday homes at towns like Los Alcázares, San Javier and Santiago de la Ribera. The seaward side of La Manga has some excellent diving areas and further south along the coast there are quiet coves.

⊞ B4　⊠ 55km east of Murcia　🍴 Restaurants and bars (€–€€€)　🚌 From Murcia　🚆 From Murcia　⛴ Excursions from Los Alcázares, Santiago de la Ribera and La Manga

Whitewashed villas scattered among the pinewoods of Moraira

MORAIRA

As much an area as a village, Moraira's name is synonymous with expensive second homes and expatriates. It lies well off the main coast road, protecting it from the crowds of some resorts. A lovely coastline, a superb 18th-century castle, good sports facilities, upmarket shops and one of Spain's best restaurants, Girasol (➤ 67), tempt visitors to return.

⊞ F2　⊠ 35km north of Benidorm　🍴 Restaurants and bars (€–€€€)

TORREVIEJA

Torrevieja's low-level houses and wide streets date from its rebuilding after a catastrophic earthquake, though older buildings survive, including the remains of the Roman port. The town is a popular holiday centre, with its beaches, sports facilities, Museo de la Semana Santa, restaurants and summer nightlife. Spanish music fans flock here in August for the Habanera Festival, a celebration of the lilting songs brought back to the town from Cuba by the 19th-century salt exporters. The salt flats at Torrevieja and La Mata are designated natural parks. Find out more at the Museo del Mar y Sal.

⊞ C3　⊠ 48km south of Alicante　🍴 Restaurants/bars (€–€€€)　🚌 From Alicante　🚆 From Alicante via Elche　⛴ To Isla de Tabarca, Cruceros Tabarca ☎ 966 70 21 22

A modern fountain in Torrevieja

VILLAJOYOSA (LA VILA JOIOSA)

'The jewelled town', with its Roman origins, started modern life as a fishing village. The old quarter is still the heart of what has become a popular holiday town, with a long sandy beach and everything for the visitor.

⊞ E2　⊠ 10km south of Benidorm　🍴 Restaurants/bars (€–€€€)　🚌 From Benidorm　🚆 From Benidorm　❓ *Moros y Cristianos* festival in Jul

Towns with Castles

PROTECTION

There are nearly 100 castles in the Costa Blanca area, most originally built by the Moors between the 8th and 13th centuries. They were designed for protection against outside threats, which ranged from tax collectors and neighbouring feudal lords to foreign invaders and pirates. Top 25 towns with castles include Alicante (➤ 25), Cocentaina (➤ 28), Dénia (➤ 29), Guadalest (➤ 33), Játiva (➤ 36) and Mula (➤ 40).

BIAR

Steeped in history and dominated by its Moorish castle, Biar is one of the most attractive of the ancient valley towns that once guarded the Castilian border. Steep, narrow streets and peaceful plazas lead up to the Castillo de Biar, with its fine valley views.

✚ C1/2 ⊠ 55km west of Alicante 🍴 Restaurants/bars (€–€€) 🚌 From Alicante 🏢 Avenida de Villena 2 ☎ 965 81 11 77 🚹 Few 🎭 Moros y Cristianos (10–13 May) **Castillo de Biar** ☎ 965 81 03 74

NOVELDA

Novelda, approached through a fertile valley planted with vines and almonds, was one of the string of important Moorish fortress towns lining the inland valleys. Outside the town rises the Castillo de la Mola, whose superb 14th-century triangular tower was designed by Ibrahim of Tunis. Stretches of ancient walling still stand. Just below is the sanctuary of Santa Magdalena, a Gaudí-influenced church. The town also has some fine Modernist houses.

✚ C2 ⊠ 30km west of Alicante 🍴 Restaurants and bars (€–€€€) 🚌 Bus from Alicante 🎭 Moros y Cristianos (19–25 Jul); Santa Magdalena (20 Jul and 7 Aug)

SAX

Sax, spreading down the hillside of the Vinalopó Valley, is one of a picturesque chain of settlements dominated by castles. The Castillo de Sax takes full advantage of its natural surroundings, the line of its walls following the contours of the limestone ridge on which it is built. The Moors built a fortress here in the 10th century. The 12th-century Levante tower survives from this era but the two courtyards and fine three-storey keep are later. Sax was finally taken by the Christians in the late 13th century.

✚ C2 ⊠ 45km west of Alicante 🍴 Restaurant/bars (€–€€) 🚌 From Alicante 🚉 From Alicante 🚹 Few 🎭 Moros y Cristianos (1–5 Feb); San Pancracio (1 May) **Castillo de Sax** ☎ 965 47 40 06

VILLENA

This lively little town, lying in the wine-producing area of the Vinalopó Valley, is dominated by La Atalaya, a square-towered 15th-century castle. The original fortress was built by the Moors as one of a chain running up the valley, but Villena's history predates the Arabs by thousands of years. The Museo Arqueológico has collections spanning 8,000 years of local history.

✚ C1 ⊠ 60km west of Alicante 🍴 Restaurants/bars (€–€€€) 🚌 From Alicante 🚉 From Alicante 🎭 Moros y Cristianos (4–9 Sep) **Museo Arqueológico** ⊠ Plaza de Santiago 2 ☎ 965 80 11 50, Ext 69 🕐 Tue–Fri 10–2, 5–8, Sat and Sun 11–1 🚹 Few 🎟 Inexpensive

The Castillo de Sax tops the rocky outcrop dominating Sax

Viewpoints & Natural Wonders

CABO DE LA NAO (CAP DE LA NAU)

The headland of Cabo de la Nao soars above the sea to
the south of Jávea (Xàbia). This stretch of coast makes
a wonderful contrast to the flat sandy beaches to the
north. Creamy white and ochre-tinted cliffs rise from
the sea, the slopes clad in pines and sweet-smelling
scrub vegetation. Unsurprisingly, the tourist boom
attracted developers, and much of the surrounding
area is dotted with secluded holiday villas. From the
cape and its lighthouse there are superb views along
the cliffs and a road leads on to the lovely cove at
Granadella (▶ 50). South of here there are no roads
and experienced walkers can enjoy the unspoilt coast.
➕ F2 ✉ 50km north of Benidorm 🍴 Restaurant and bars (€–€€)
♿ Few

CABO DE SAN MARTÍN (CAP DE SANT MARTÍ)

The beautiful bay of Jávea is sheltered at its southern
end by the Cabo de San Martín, a rocky promontory
where it is easy to escape the crowds of the nearby
beaches. South of Jávea a path drops from the road at
the Cruz de Portichol, a stone wayside cross from
where both the cape and the island of Portichol (Isla
de Portitxol) are visible. This leads out to San Martín,
running through clumps of lavender, thyme and
rosemary, to emerge at the headland. The all-round
views are excellent. Other tracks lead up and down the
coast, one to Cala Sardinera (▶ 50).
➕ F2 ✉ 50km north of Benidorm ♿ None

COLL DE RATES

The Coll de Rates road (▶ 17) is one of the most
scenic on the Costa Blanca. The road climbs and twists
steadily through mountain scenery to the pass, which
lies at 780m. From the north the rise is gradual, the
fertile agricultural plain dropping away and the
vegetation changing as views of the sea emerge.
Through the *coll*, the southern landscape is enclosed
by the dramatic Parcent and Aixorta mountains.
➕ E2 ✉ 40km north of Benidorm 🍴 Restaurants and bars en route
(€–€€€)

CUEVA DE CANALOBRE (COVES DE CANELOBRE)

The hills of Cabeçó d'Or, north of Alicante, are riddled
with caves and grottoes. This impressive limestone
cavern, with one of the highest vaults in Spain, has
been skilfully illuminated to show off the stalactites,
stalagmites and strange limestone formations.
➕ D2 ✉ 24km north of Alicante and 40km southwest of Benidorm
☎ 965 69 92 50 🕐 20 Jun–1 Oct daily 10:30–7:45; 2 Oct–19 Jun
daily 11–5:45 🍴 Restaurant and bar (€–€€) ♿ Few
❓ Concerts are sometimes held in the cave in summer; details from
local tourist offices

*The rocky island of
Portichol, seen from the
wooded headland of
Cabo de San Martín*

Churches & Monasteries

DUAL ROLE

The oval interior of Murcia's flamboyant baroque San Juan de Dios has doubled up as both church and museum for some years. Catholic Mass is celebrated every Sunday, but for the rest of the week the church acts as an elegant ecclesiastical backdrop for a fine collection of religious imagery, including works by artists such as Salzillo, Beltrán and Bussy.

➕ A3 ✉ Eulogio Soriano 4
☎ 968 21 45 41 ⏰ Tue–Fri 10–2, 5–8:30, Sat, Sun, 10–2. Closed Aug ♿ Few 💶 Free

Alicante's 17th-century Concatedral de San Nicolás de Bari

In the Top 25
14 JÁTIVA'S SAN FELIU (➤ 37)
15 MURCIA'S SANTA MARÍA (➤ 42)

CATEDRAL, ORIHUELA

This cathedral, with its nearby 18th-century bishop's palace, started life as a simple church, built between 1305 and 1355. Over the centuries alterations and additions have produced a wonderful mixture of styles, ranging from Romanesque through Catalan Gothic to baroque. The vaulted transept, built in 1500, is a high point, its bizarre, spirally twisted ribs rising to the shadows of the roof. More embellishments followed after the church became a cathedral in 1564. The serene two-storey cloister, its honey-coloured arches enclosing a trim garden, was moved here after the Civil War. It contains the Museo Diocesano del Arte Sacro, with Velázquez's *The Temptation of St Thomas*.

➕ B3 ✉ Plaza Teniente Linares s/n ⏰ Mon–Fri 10:30–1:30, 5:30–7:30, Sat 10:30–1:30 💶 Free ♿ Good **Museo Diocesano del Arte Sacro** ⏰ Same as cathedral 💶 Inexpensive

CONCATEDRAL DE SAN NICOLÁS DE BARI, ALICANTE

The cathedral was built between 1616 and 1662 to replace the 13th-century church that stood on the site of the city's mosque. The façade is simple Renaissance in style, but the interior, with its soaring dome, is closer to baroque, heavy with carving and gilt. The 15th-century cloister provides an effective contrast.

➕ D2 ✉ Plaza Abad Penalva 1 ☎ 965 21 26 62 ⏰ Daily 6–7:30PM (and during mass) 🚌 G, H, M ♿ Good 💶 Free

IGLESIA DE SANTA MARÍA, ALICANTE

Alicante's oldest church was built in the 14th century on the site of a mosque in the heart of the original Arab town. It has been frequently altered and is today a marvellous *mélange* of different architectural styles. The great golden altar dates from the late 1400s and the font from the following century.

➕ D2 ✉ Plaza de Santa María ☎ 965 21 60 26 ⏰ Daily 10:30–1, 7–7:30 🚌 G, H, M, P, S ♿ Few 💶 Free

MURCIA'S CHURCHES

Murcia is full of ecclesiastical architecture and fans of the baroque will find many examples of this exuberant style. Among the best churches are La Merced, San Miguel, Santa Ana and Santa Clara, grouped together on the edge of the old town. All have superb façades and Salzillo carvings inside. Another good trio is San Pedro, San Nicolás and Santa Catalina, nearby.

➕ A3 ⏰ Daily 9–1, 5–7 💶 Free

Museums

CARTAGENA'S MUSEUMS
The first impression of Cartagena is of a rather run-down industrial city with a naval dockyard and modern suburbs. But it's worth persevering, as the old city has some of Murcia's best museums. The Museo Arqueológico Municipal traces the city's history and has a large Roman collection. The Museo Nacional de Arqueología Marítima has shipwreck finds and a replica of a Roman galley.

🔲 A4 ☒ 53km southeast of Murcia 🚌 From Murcia 🚆 From Murcia 🛈 Puertas de San José, Plaza Bastarreche ☎ 968 50 64 83 **Museo Arqueológico Municipal** ☒ Ramón y Cajal 45 ☎ 968 12 88 81 🕐 Tue–Fri 10–2, 5–8, Sat and Sun 11–2 🚻 Few 🏷 Free **Museo Nacional de Arqueología Marítima** ☒ Dique de Navidad s/n ☎ 968 12 11 66 🕐 Tue–Sun 10–3 🚻 Few 🏷 Free

MUSEO DE BELLAS ARTES, MURCIA
A large and variable collection of pictures giving a comprehensive view of the development of Murcian painting from the 15th to the 20th centuries.

🔲 A3 ☒ Obispo Frutos 12 ☎ 968 23 93 46 🕐 Mon–Fri 9–2, 5–8, Sat 10–2 (summer 9–1) 🚻 Good 🏷 Moderate

MUSEO SALZILLO, MURCIA
Murcia's most important museum displays work by the 18th-century wood sculptor Francisco Salzillo, born in the city. He specialised in dramatic and detailed polychrome figures and scenes from the life of Christ. Most of these were designed to be carried through the streets during the Holy Week processions, as indeed they are still. Don't miss the nativity scene, with over 500 rustic figures.

🔲 A3 ☒ Plaza San Agustín 3 ☎ 968 29 18 93 🕐 Sep–Jun Tue–Sat 9:30–1, 4–7, Sun 11–1; Jul–Aug, Mon–Fri 9:30–1, 4–7 🚻 Few 🏷 Moderate

MUSEO MUNICIPAL DE ALMUDÍN, JÁTIVA
Housed in the mid-16th-century municipal granary, Játiva's town museum is worth a visit for the building alone. The Gothic façade hides a spacious Renaissance interior built around a graceful columned courtyard, all imaginatively restored as a backdrop for the collections. The exhibits include Iberian and Roman artefacts and Moorish ceramics. There are paintings by José de Ribera (▶ 9) and a loan collection of mainly 17th-century works from the Prado in Madrid. Look for the Goya engravings and the portrait of Philip V, hung upside down in retribution for his burning of Játiva during the War of the Spanish Succession.

🔲 D1 ☒ Corretgeria 46 ☎ 962 27 65 97 🕐 Mid-Sep to mid-Jun, Tue–Fri 10–2, 4–6, Sat and Sun 10–2; mid-Jun to mid-Sep, Tue–Sun 10–2 🚻 Good 🏷 Moderate

WINE MUSEUMS
Wine buffs should visit Jumilla, a small agricultural and market town, well off the beaten track, in the rolling sierras of Murcia's northern corner. Its vineyards were first planted by the Romans and are among Europe's oldest. You can learn more in the idiosyncratic Museo del Vino before a visit to the Franciscan monastery and its little Museo Jerónimo Molina.

🔲 A2 ☒ 55km north of Murcia **Juan Carcelén Museo del Vino** ☒ García Lorca 1 ☎ 968 75 60 64 for an apppointment **Museo Jerónimo Molina** ☒ Plaza de la Constitución 3 ☎ 968 78 07 40 🕐 Tue–Sat 9–1, 4–7, Sun 10–1

FIESTA TIME
The industrial town of Alcoy (Alcoi) has the fascinating Museo de Fiestas, where the costumes used in the *Moros y Christianos* festival are stored.

🔲 D1 ☒ San Miguel 60 🕐 Tue–Fri 11:30–1:30, 5:30–7:30, Sat, Sun 11:30–1:30

Murcia's Museo Salzillo

Attractions for Kids

The Costa Blanca Express travels up the coast from Alicante to Dénia

Playing in the sand on Benidorm's Playa de Levante

ALICANTE (ALACANT)
Costa Blanca Express
This narrow-gauge train ambles up the coast from Alicante to Dénia, stopping en route.
➕ D2 ✉ Alicante ☎ 965 26 27 31; ➕ E2 ✉ Benidorm ☎ 965 85 18 95; ➕ F1 ✉ Dénia ☎ 965 78 04 45 ⏰ 6AM–9PM

TORREVIEJA
Aquapolis
A big aquapark with pools, hydrotubs and plenty of slides and rides, water mountains and artificial waves.
➕ C3 ✉ Finca la Olla Grande s/n ☎ 965 71 58 90 ⏰ Mid-Jun to mid-Sep 11–7 🍴 Restaurants and a picnic area

BENIDORM
Aqualandia
The biggest, best-known and most popular aquapark in Benidorm. Plenty of rides, slides and pools.
➕ E2 ✉ Sierra Helada, Partida Bayo ☎ 965 86 01 00 ⏰ May to mid-Oct 11–7 🚌 2, 7

Barco a la Isla
Enjoy a boat trip out to Benidorm Island, a nature reserve just off the coast, in a glass-bottomed boat.
➕ E2 ✉ Puerto de Benidorm ☎ 965 85 00 52

Festilandia
A good amusement park for very small children.
➕ E2 ✉ Avenida del Mediterráneo 20 ☎ 965 85 41 26 ☎ 11–7

Karting la Cala
A chance for older children to test their skill and nerves on one of Europe's largest go-karting tracks.
➕ E2 ✉ Avenida Villaiosa 11 ☎ 965 89 46 76 ⏰ Winter 11–7; summer 11–8

Mundomar
A marine park beside Aqualandia with a dolphin show, seals, parrots and a maze of wooded paths and water features to explore.
➕ E2 ✉ Sierra Helada, Rincón de Loix ☎ 965 86 91 01 ⏰ 10–6 🚌 2, 7

Museo de Cera
Wax figures of Spanish and international personalities.
➕ E2 ✉ Avenida Mediterráneo 8 ☎ 966 80 84 21 ⏰ 10–7 🚌 2

Terra Mítica
The 'World of Myth' theme park has rides and shows in five areas based on past Mediterranean civilisations – Egypt, Greece, Rome, Iberia and the Islands.
➕ E2 ✉ Ctra Benidorm a Finestrat, Camino del Moralet s/n ☎ 966 83 51 86 ⏰ Summer 10AM–midnight; mid Sep–Oct 10–8; winter 10–6

CALPE (CALP)
Aquascope
Trips around the Peñón de Ifach in a semi-submersible boat with an underwater glass observation chamber.
➕ F2 ✉ Puerto de Calpe ☎ 965 83 85 32 🕒 Summer

GUADALEST
Museo del Juguete Antiguo 1790–1959
A toy museum with an enormous collection from all over the world.
➕ E2 ✉ Guadalest ☎ 965 88 52 66 🕒 10–7 🚌 From Benidorm

JÁTIVA (XÀTIVA)
El Castell
The ultimate in castles, complete with towers, look-out points, cannons and walkways.
➕ D1 ✉ Carretera Castillo ☎ 962 27 42 74 🕒 Summer Tue–Sun 10–7; winter 10–6

PENAGUILA
Safari Aitana
A safari park in the Aitana Sierra with lions, giraffes, elephants and other animals. It's a good choice in hot weather, as you can swim in the pool.
➕ E2 ✉ Carretera Villajoyosa (La Vila Joiosa)–Benidorm ☎ 965 52 92 73 🕒 11–6:30

VERGEL (VERGER)
Safari Park Vergel
A drive-round safari park near the beaches; also has a dolphin show.
➕ F1 ✉ Carretera Vergel–Pego ☎ 965 75 02 85 🕒 10–5:45

CARTAGENA
Museo Nacional de Arqueología Marítima
Treasures from the seabed, including a reconstruction of a perfectly loaded ship (▶ 57).
➕ A4 ✉ Dique de Navidad s/n, Puerto de Cartagena ☎ 968 12 11 68 🕒 Tue–Sat 9:30–3, Sun 10–3

LA MANGA
Excursiones Joven Maria Dolores
Daily boat trips out to the islands in the Mar Menor.
➕ B4 ✉ From Santiago de la Ribera and Los Alcázares ☎ 629 60 71 47 🕒 15 Jun–30 Sep. Groups in winter by appointment only

MURCIA
Museo de la Ciencia
A good science museum, with water as its main theme. Many hands-on exhibits and a children's planetarium.
➕ A3 ✉ Plaza de la Ciencia 1 ☎ 968 21 19 98 🕒 Tue–Fri 10–1, 4–8; Sat 10–2, 5–8; Sun 11–2 🚌 7a

---

CHILDREN WELCOME

Spaniards love children and make them welcome everywhere. Local kids stay up late so there is no need to leave yours at home in the evenings. They will be welcome at all but the grandest restaurants. Encourage them to say *hola* (hello) and *gracias* (thank you), two words which go a long way to winning local hearts.

Places to Relax

FORTUNA

A few kilometres outside the workaday town of Fortuna lies the Balneario, one of Murcia's handful of thermal hot springs. Used by the Romans and Arabs, the water quality is among the best in Europe for rheumatic and respiratory complaints. The spa's layout today dates from the late 19th century, with an atmospheric group of dignified hotels set around palm-shaded promenades. Deep below lies the spring itself, gushing out at a temperature of 53°C, and channelled directly into the treatment rooms. Here you can wallow in a marble bath with water up to your neck or enjoy a range of showers and massages. If this sounds daunting, there are plenty of other facilities, including a steaming open-air swimming pool fed by the springs.

➕ A3 ✉ 22km north of Murcia ⏰ Baths and treatments: daily 8–1PM; swimming pool: 10–9 ☎ 968 68 50 11 🍴 Restaurant and bar (€–€€) 🚌 From Murcia 🚉 From Murcia ♿ Excellent 💷 Moderate

Above: *taking a break in the spa town of Fortuna*
Below: *the stunning Fuentes del Algar*

LA ISLA DE BENIDORM

A mere 20-minute boat trip across the bay, Benidorm Island makes a good destination for a picnic and swim. Rising at one end to sheer cliffs, its clear deep waters are ideal for snorkelling and scuba diving. The island is uninhabited except for seabirds, and is a designated sanctuary. You can get there in an 'aquascope' boat, whose transparent hull lets you see underwater.

➕ E2 🍴 Summer-only bar 🚢 Excursiones Maritimo, Puerto de Benidorm ☎ 965 85 00 52 ⏰ Every 45 minutes 10–6

FUENTES DEL ALGAR (FONTS DE L'ALGAR)

The river Algar flows down from the high sierras behind the Benidorm coast. Its waterfalls are a tourist honeypot. A series of crystal-clear cascades has been landscaped and attracts countless visitors who enjoy the waterside paths and bathe in the pools. The approach to this spot, through the hills and loquat plantations, is beautiful. The sight and sound of water on a hot summer day is enchanting, and the Museo de Medio Ambiente (environmental museum) and aromatic plant collection are added attractions.

➕ E2 ✉ 16km from Benidorm 🍴 Bars and restaurants nearby (€–€€) 🔄 Guadalest (▶ 33) **Museo de Medio Ambiente** ☎ 965 97 21 29 ⏰ 9–6 ♿ Few 💷 Moderate

COSTA BLANCA
where to...

Alicante (Alacant)

PRICES

Prices are approximate, based on the cost of a three-course meal for one, without drinks or service.

€ = up to €10
€€ = €10–€20
€€€ = over €20

EAT SPANISH

You will find a huge variety of places, ranging from cheap-and-cheerful to restaurants whose style – and costs – rival top international restaurants anywhere. Those listed here mainly offer Spanish and local specialities, which might be more difficult to track down on your own.

It is quite acceptable in Spain to have one course and a salad, so do not think you have to wade through the whole menu.

AZAHAR (€€€)

The chef and maître d' from one of Alicante's oldest restaurants branched out here on their own, and the years of experience certainly show in the excellent cooking and attention to detail.
✉ C/ Alberola 57 ☎ 965 12 13 48 🕐 Lunch daily, Fri and Sat lunch and dinner

EL BOCAITO (€€)

Atmospheric and lively bar and restaurant, serving tapas and a good range of dishes with the emphasis on rice and shellfish.
✉ Isabel la Católica 22 ☎ 965 92 26 30 🕐 Lunch and dinner. Closed Sun

CÉSAR ANCA (€€)

A friendly pub-style restaurant, where the simple, appetising food is prepared with an up-to-date twist. Excellent service by more waiters than in many grander establishments.
✉ General Lacy 12 ☎ 965 92 26 30 🕐 Closed Mon PM, Sun and all Jul

LOS CHARROS (€)

A great lunchtime choice at the Playa de San Juan. This attractive bar-restaurant serves up the best tapas and traditional dishes among the bars in this part of town.
✉ Avenida de Bruselas 15 ☎ 965 21 32 14 🕐 Lunch daily

DARSENA (€€€)

An elegant restaurant in the marina with the emphasis firmly on *arroces*, seafood and fish. Service can be a bit chaotic at busy times and the wine list can err towards fashion rather than quality.
✉ Muelle de Levante 6, Marina Deportiva ☎ 965 20 75 89 🕐 Lunch, dinner. Closed Sun PM

GRILL SANT JUAN (€€€)

A hotel restaurant with a terrace, specialising in traditional Spanish cuisine. Wonderful service, excellent wine list.
✉ La Doblada s/n ☎ 965 16 13 00 🕐 Lunch and dinner

EL JARDIN DE GALICIA (€€€)

In the heart of Alicante, specialising in cooking from Galicia, from where much of the excellent meat and shellfish comes.
✉ Maisonnave 33 ☎ 965 12 01 61 🕐 Lunch and dinner. Closed Sun

JUMILLANO (€€€)

This long-established *méson*-style restaurant began in the 1930s as a wine and oil shop – today it's one of the city's finest places to eat, serving impeccably cooked and presented local dishes.
✉ César Elguezábal 62 ☎ 965 21 29 64 🕐 Closed Sun PM

LO DE REME (€€)

A family restaurant with imaginative cooking; serving *bacalao* (dried cod) and liver and kidney dishes.
✉ Isabel la Católica 6 ☎ 965 12 39 02 🕐 Lunch and dinner. Closed Sun and Mon, and Wed PM

EL LUGAR (€)

Good local cooking using the freshest ingredients.

The food is very good quality and value for money. Popular with locals.

✉ García Morato 4 ☎ 965 14 11 31 🕐 Lunch and dinner. Closed Sun and holidays

MAESTRAL (€€)

An old-established upmarket restaurant, one of the first to open in the early tourist years, specialising in rice dishes and shellfish, as well as some international specialities.

✉ Andalucía 18 ☎ 965 16 46 18 🕐 Lunch and dinner. Closed Sun PM

MIXTO VEGETARIANO (€)

Earthy hole-in-the-wall restaurant with vegetarian dishes and outside seating on a pretty square.

✉ Plaza de Santa Maria 2 ☎ None 🕐 Lunch and dinner. Closed Mon

NOU MANOLIN (€€)

Very popular bar and restaurant serving the best of Alicante and Spanish cooking. Rice and shellfish, with good wine list.

✉ Villegas 3 ☎ 965 20 03 68 🕐 Lunch and dinner

ONE-ONE (€€)

Idiosyncratic restaurant with a French twist. No menus, just what looked good in the market that day, all served with panache and style.

✉ Valdés 9 ☎ 965 20 63 99 🕐 Lunch and dinner. Closed Sun and Mon

PACHÀ (€€)

A good range of rice dishes, as well as braised

meat and tasty fish, served in a traditional setting.

✉ Haroldo Parrés 6 ☎ 965 21 19 38 🕐 Lunch and dinner. Closed Wed and Sun PM

PEKIN (€)

Peking-style cooking with the usual set meals or *à la carte*. Good downtown choice.

✉ Reyes Católicos 57 ☎ 965 92 98 67 🕐 Lunch and dinner

PIRIPI (€€)

Rice is cooked to perfection in this friendly family-run restaurant. A huge range of tapas.

✉ Oscar Esplá 30 ☎ 965 22 79 40 🕐 Lunch and dinner

RACÓ DEL PLA (€€)

An excellent rice and fish restaurant, where the owners take pride in the freshness of their ingredients.

✉ Dr Nieto 42 ☎ 965 21 93 73 🕐 Lunch and dinner. Closed second two weeks in Aug

TRAGALLUM (€€)

The chef makes full use of local ingredients and traditions. Dishes include rabbit with pine-nuts and parsley, and fine terrines spiked with rosemary.

✉ Campo Vassallo 33 ☎ 965 21 38 69 🕐 Lunch and dinner. Closed Sun PM and Mon

VALENCIA 11 (€)

Good-value bar-restaurant offering Alicante dishes and some of the best puddings in town. Very popular, so it's best to book.

✉ Valencia 11 ☎ 965 21 13 09 🕐 Lunch and dinner. Closed Sun and Mon PM, Easter week and mid-Aug to mid-Sep

TAPAS

Tapas bars abound all over Spain, and are an excellent way to feel the spirit of a city. Don't be put off by dark interiors – these are often the best. You'll find them well patronised by locals having a quick snack with a glass of wine or beer. The dishes themselves range from olives and almonds to *tortilla, jamón serrano*, shellfish, anchovies, meat croquettes and wonderful vegetable dishes, laced with chilli and garlic. The cold tapas are displayed at the counter and the hot ones cooked to order. *Raciones* are bigger servings than *porciones*. Two or three will be plenty for lunch and a truly Spanish experience.

Around Alicante

BUDGET EATING

The resorts of the Costa Blanca have such a wide range of restaurants that it's easy to find one to suit every pocket. For inexpensive eating you can head for a tapas bar or try the food on offer in a *cervecería* or *bodega*. These usually serve *platos combinados*, literally a combination plate, which should satisfy the healthiest appetite. One of these, followed by a visit to a *heladería* (ice-cream bar), provides a good simple meal.

A SWEET TOOTH

Jijona (Xixona) is the place to go if you have a sweet tooth. This everyday little town, in the sierras behind Alicante, is the home of *turrón*, an almond and honey-based nougat traditionally eaten at Christmas. Probably of Moorish origin, *turrón* is still produced by more than 30 small-scale family businesses on an artisan basis. There is a bewildering variety to choose from, ranging from soft and gooey to slightly crisp and tooth-cracking caramel.

CARTAGENA

VENTA VISTA ALEGRE (€€)
Situated between Alicante and Cartagena, this popular roadside restaurant serves up a delicious mixed grill of fish and seafood.
✉ Alicante–Cartagena km89 ☎ 965 41 10 02 🕐 Lunch and dinner

ELCHE (ELX)

ASADOR ILICITANO (€€)
If Valencian fare is beginning to pall, head for this rustic-style restaurant for a taste of Castile – huge roasts (including suckling pig), hearty bean dishes and fine hams, as well as fish dishes.
✉ Maestro Giner 9 ☎ 965 43 58 64 🕐 Lunch and dinner. Closed Sun and 15–30 Aug

DOÑA ANA (€)
Come to this bastion of traditional cooking to enjoy succulent grilled meats, fish and shellfish. On weekdays they also offer a good-value *menú del día*.
✉ Dr Caro 17 ☎ 965 44 44 94 🕐 Lunch and dinner. Closed Sun

LA FINCA (€€€)
Good grills, fish and game dishes and a terrace for summer eating. Much-patronised by local businessmen. Service can be slow.
✉ Partida Perleta 1 ☎ 965 45 60 07 🕐 Lunch and dinner. Closed Sun PM, Mon and three weeks in Jan

PARQUE MUNICIPAL (€)
Big, busy restaurant in the centre of Elche's palm forest. The décor is functional but the food is spot-on; a good place to eat *arroz con costra*.
✉ Paseo Estacion s/n ☎ 965 45 34 15 🕐 Lunch and dinner

GUARDAMAR DEL SEGURA

RINCÓN DE PEDRO (€)
A cheerful, lively atmosphere, big terrace and good range of rice and fish dishes.
✉ Cibeles 2, Urbanización las Dunas ☎ 965 72 80 95 🕐 Lunch and dinner. Closed Wed

MONÓVAR (MONÒVER)

CASA ELIAS (€€)
A good place to sample some inland rice dishes and traditional, country-style home cooking.
✉ Rosales 7, Cinorlet ☎ 966 97 95 17 🕐 Lunch only. Closed Wed

XIRI (€€)
The food has character and uses fresh local ingredients. Excellent selection of local wines.
✉ Parque Alameda s/n ☎ 965 47 29 10 🕐 Lunch and dinner. Closed Sun PM, Mon and 20 Feb–15 Mar

ORIHUELA

EUROPA (€)
Solid home-style cooking at this no-frills restaurant conveniently located in the centre of town.
✉ Plaza Europa ☎ 966 74 26 78 🕐 Lunch and dinner. Closed Sun and Aug

CASA CORRO (€)

Functional but excellent restaurant near the palm forest, with the accent on regional cooking.

✉ Avenida García Rogel s/n, Palmeral de San Antón ☎ 965 30 29 63 🕐 Lunch and dinner. Closed Mon PM and second two weeks of Aug

SANTA POLA

BATISTE (€€)

A pretty restaurant in a flower-filled garden beside the sea, offering shellfish, rice and fish, and an excellent wine list.

✉ Pérez Ojeda 6 ☎ 965 41 14 85 🕐 Lunch and dinner

LA GOLETA (€€)

A nautically themed tavern offering great rice recipes from Tabarca. The fish and shellfish are wonderfully fresh. There is a lively atmosphere.

✉ Hernán Cortés 6 ☎ 966 69 30 63 🕐 Lunch and dinner. Closed Mon (except Jul and Aug), and two weeks in Oct/Nov

MIRAMAR (€€)

An elegant summer restaurant with a big terrace and friendly service. Local rice and fish, with lots of vegetables and the freshest of salads.

✉ Pérez Ojeda 8 ☎ 965 41 10 00 🕐 Lunch and dinner

PALOMAR (€€)

Enjoy the best of local rice and seafood dishes beside the beach on the terrace of this bustling restaurant.

✉ Playa de Levante s/n ☎ 965 41 32 00 🕐 Lunch and dinner

TORREVIEJA

BAHÍA (€)

Good range of seafood and international dishes.

✉ Avenida Libertad 3 ☎ 965 71 39 94 🕐 Lunch and dinner. Closed Mon

BRISAS DEL MAR (€)

Popular restaurant with terrace; some unusual local dishes.

✉ Paseo Vista Alegre 10 ☎ 965 70 52 01 🕐 Lunch and dinner. Closed Mon PM

CABO ROIG (€€)

Pleasantly situated eatery with a summer terrace.

✉ Urbanización Cabo Roig s/n, Carretera Torrevieja–Cartagena Km 8 ☎ 966 76 02 90 🕐 Lunch and dinner

RESTAURANTE VEGETARIANO (€€)

Imaginative vegetarian restaurant run by a Spanish –Australian couple.

✉ Calle Pedro Lorca 13 ☎ 966 70 66 83 🕐 Lunch and dinner. Closed Mon

VILLENA

LA TEJA AZUL (€€)

Cosy rustic feel with brick and beam interior. There are a range of filling rice dishes, including the house speciality, *arroz a banda*.

✉ Calle Sancho Medina 34 ☎ 965 34 82 34 🕐 Lunch and dinner. Closed Tue

WARY NESSY (€)

Excellent family-run restaurant specialising in dishes peculiar to Villena.

✉ Isabel la Católica 13A ☎ 965 80 10 47 🕐 Lunch and dinner. Closed Mon and second two weeks in Jul

VEGETARIAN EATING

Although Spaniards do not really understand vegetarianism, if you eat fish you will find possibilities on every menu. If not, the range of vegetable dishes available is huge, particularly in Murcia. Salads appear everywhere and it is quite acceptable to ask for a *tortilla*, the classic potato and onion omelette. Country places often have wonderful local vegetable stews and soups, cheese is good and some rice dishes have no meat or fish in them. If you are staying in the Benidorm area, an excellent restaurant is Restaurante Vegetariano in Torrevieja (see listing), which has a wide range of vegetarian choices, and meat and fish dishes as well.

Benidorm & the North

VENTURING FORTH

The chances are your holiday price will include three meals a day, but make a point of splashing out on one or two restaurant meals to ensure you sample some really local dishes. Restaurants offer a three-course *menú del día* (menu of the day), which will often feature rice and fish dishes and be generally good value. The smaller the restaurant the higher the chance of finding real Spanish food. The buzz of Spanish voices will tell you if you're on the right track. Many menus feature illustrations of the various specialities, so you shouldn't have a language problem.

BENIDORM

L'ALBUFERA (€)
This popular restaurant is busy all day, thanks to the great range of tapas, good-value *menús* and splendid rice dishes.
✉ Gerona 3 ☎ 965 86 56 61 🕐 Lunch and dinner

LA PALMERA-CASA PACO NADAL (€€)
One of Benidorm's oldest restaurants, specialising in fish and rice dishes.
✉ Avenida Dr Severo Ochoa 44, Rincón de Loix ☎ 965 85 32 82 🕐 Lunch only except Jul–Aug. Closed Mon

EL PULPO PIRATA (€)
A restaurant and bar near the old quarter, popular with local people. Range of excellent-value dishes and tapas and a tiny shady terrace for eating alfresco.
✉ Calle Tomás Ortuño s/n ☎ 966 80 32 19 🕐 Lunch and dinner

RÍAS BAIXAS (€€)
Grab a terrace table at this big, functional restaurant where you can sample plain grilled fish, excellent shellfish and some more international dishes.
✉ Plaza Torrechó 3 ☎ 965 85 50 22 🕐 Lunch and dinner. Closed Mon

ALTEA

MONTEMOLAR (€€€)
Slightly ostentatious but elegant restaurant. Fresh produce, caviar, Scottish salmon and fillet steak.
✉ Monte Molar 38 ☎ 965 84 15 81 🕐 Dinner only (except Sun). Closed Wed and Jan–Mar

EL PATIO (€€)
Eat in a cool shady garden. Specialities include paella, *fideuà*, *arroz a la banda* and the freshest of grilled fish.
✉ Avenida del Puerto 9 ☎ 965 84 39 89 🕐 Lunch and dinner. Closed Thu and Nov–Feb

SANT PERE 23 (€€)
Enjoy a special seafood moment at this beachfront restaurant, popular with locals.
✉ Calle San Pedro 24 ☎ 965 84 49 72 🕐 Lunch and dinner

CABO DE LA NAO (CAP DE LA NAU)

CABO LA NAU (€€)
Perched on a high headland with splendid views. Good tapas, rice and fish and a pretty outside terrace.
✉ Faro Cabo de la Nau, Jávea ☎ 965 77 18 35 🕐 Lunch and dinner. Closed Wed

CALPE (CALP)

CASA FLORENCIA (€€)
Tucked away in one of the most attractive corners of old Calpe, this restaurant serves good Valencian cooking.
✉ Plaça del Mariners ☎ 965 83 35 84 🕐 Lunch and dinner. Closed Sun

INTERNACIONAL (€€)
Right on the beach, the Internacional has a big airy dining room and a splendid terrace. Choose from the à la carte menu or good-value *menú del día*.
✉ Edificio Aguamarina, Playa de Levante ☎ 965 83 60 03 🕐 9AM–midnight. Closed Jan and Feb

DÉNIA

EL ASADOR DEL PUERTO (€€)
The accent is firmly on meat, including game in season.
✉ Plaça del Raset 10–11
☎ 966 42 34 82 🕒 Lunch, dinner

EL RASET (€€€)
One of Dénia's oldest and smartest restaurants, in the fishing quarter.
✉ Bellaviata 7 ☎ 965 78 50 40 🕒 Lunch and dinner

GANDÍA

EMILIO (€€)
Sophisticated restaurant near the beach. Great use is made of fresh market produce; a good choice for something a bit special.
✉ B Bloque F-5, Av Vicente Calderón ☎ 962 84 07 61
🕒 Lunch and dinner. Closed Wed except Jul and Aug

GUADALEST

VENTA LA MONTAÑA (€€)
An inn with a terrace, opened in 1910, and still going strong. Dishes typical of this area.
✉ Carretera Alcoy 9, Benimantell ☎ 965 88 51 41
🕒 Lunch and dinner in summer, dinner only in winter. Closed Mon except in Aug

JÁTIVA (XÀTIVA)

CASA LA ABUELA (€€€)
Excellent restaurant offering local recipes. Look out for *arnadí*, a rich cake made with pumpkin, almonds and pine-nuts.
✉ Reina 17 ☎ 962 28 10 85

🕒 Lunch and dinner. Closed Sun, and mid-Jun to mid Aug

JÁVEA (XÀBIA)

CRISTÓBAL COLÓN (€€)
Right on the promenade with a vast terrace. Excellently prepared rice and fish dishes.
✉ Playa de Arena ☎ 966 47 09 58 🕒 Lunch and dinner

TASCA TONIS (€)
The locals' favourite, so it's busy year-round. Home-cooking at its best, using local ingredients.
✉ Mayor 2 ☎ 966 46 18 51
🕒 Lunch, dinner. Closed Sun PM

MORAIRA

GIRASOL (€€€)
A pretty chalet with a terrace, considered the foremost restaurant in Valencia and one of the best in Spain.
✉ Carretera Moraira–Calpe km 1.5 ☎ 965 74 43 73
🕒 Lunch and dinner (except in summer when PM only Tue–Sat). Closed Mon

SELLA

BAR FONDA (€)
Serving good country dishes, this is popular with locals, so book in advance.
✉ Carretera Alcoy 15 ☎ 965 87 90 11 🕒 Lunch and dinner

VILLAJOYOSA (LA VILA JOIOSA)

CASA ELORDI (€€)
A pretty old house in the historic quarter. Head for the palm-shaded terrace.
✉ Puerta Dr Esquerdo 8
☎ 966 85 26 63 🕒 Lunch and dinner. Closed Sun

ARROZ

Arroz, or rice, is the staple in this area, and is found up and down the Costa Blanca. It grows all over the region, but the most famous comes from the inland town of Calasparra, high in the Segura valley, and is one of Spain's few foods with a *denominación de origen*. Spanish rice has a nutty, intense flavour and a good bite even when cooked. To taste it at its best it must be served as soon as it is cooked, steaming and aromatic with the fish, meat and vegetables that flavour it. To enjoy the real thing, sample it in a restaurant that specialises in *arroces*, and make sure the menu advises a 20-minute wait – the time it takes to cook rice to perfection.

Murcia

THE *HUERTA*

Look on a pack of vegetables in your supermarket at home and the chances are high that the producer's address will be in Murcia. The fertile flatlands, the *huerta* (garden), around the city were first cultivated by the Moors and have produced intensely flavoured, tender young vegetables and a range of fruit for centuries. With the advent of rapid refrigerated transport, the industry boomed and today the *huerta* supplies many northern European markets. Much produce still stays at home, though, providing the raw ingredients for the huge range of delicious and imaginative vegetable dishes that are an essential part of Murcian cooking.

MURCIA

EL CHURRA (€)
A pretty hotel restaurant serving classic Murcian recipes, with a range of vegetable specialities, plus excellent grilled steaks and a comprehensive wine list.
✉ Avenida Marqués de los Vélez 12 ☎ 968 23 84 00 🕐 Lunch and dinner

EL FELIPE (€€)
Genuine Murcian vegetable and egg-based specialities at reasonable prices, as well as meat and fish, at this friendly restaurant across the river from the cathedral.
✉ C/ González Adalid 11 ☎ 968 21 20 66 🕐 Lunch, dinner. Closed Sun PM and Aug

HISPANO (€€)
Murcian-style restaurant, with outstanding vegetable dishes and excellent fish. Good wine list and attentive service.
✉ Arquitecto Cerdá 3 ☎ 968 21 61 52 🕐 Lunch and dinner. Closed Sat in Jul and Aug

MESÓN EL CORRAL (€€)
Right in the heart of the old town and decorated with hand-painted *azulejos*, this friendly restaurant offers an enormous range of tapas as well as a full menu.
✉ Plaza Santo Domingo 23–24 ☎ 968 21 45 97/21 49 85 🕐 Lunch and dinner

LA ONDA (€€€)
A cool and elegant restaurant serving fish and meat dishes and Murcian vegetable specialities.

Range of wines.
✉ Bando de la Huerta 8 ☎ 968 24 78 82 🕐 Lunch and dinner. Closed Sun and 15 days in Aug

RINCÓN DEL PEPE (€€€)
The restaurant (in a hotel of the same name) that put traditional Murcian cooking firmly on the Spanish gastronomic map. Wonderful local vegetable, meat and fish dishes and a superb wine selection.
✉ Apóstoles 34 ☎ 968 21 22 39 🕐 Lunch and dinner. Closed Sun PM

ROCÍO (€€)
Restaurant on the edge of the historic centre started by two chefs formerly at the famous Rincón del Pepe (above), serving similar Murcian dishes at half the price. Worth seeking out.
✉ Batalla de las Flores s/n ☎ 968 24 29 30 🕐 Lunch and dinner. Closed Sun

ÁGUILAS

LAS BRISAS (€€)
Maritime-themed restaurant serving fresh fish and rice dishes. Try the huge prawns or crayfish or the light-as-a-feather *fritura de pascado*.
✉ Explanda del Puerto s/n ☎ 968 41 00 27 🕐 Lunch and dinner. Closed Mon

EL ALGAR

LOS CHURRASCOS (€€)
One of the region's best restaurants, rustically decorated. Superb meat and fish; renowned wine list.

✉ Avenida Filipinas 13 ☎ 968 13 61 44 🕐 Lunch and dinner. Closed Mon

CABO DE PALOS

MIRAMAR (€€)

Big functional restaurant in a wonderful position beside the sea, renowned for its freshest of fish and lightest of frying.

✉ Paeso de la Barra 14 ☎ 968 56 30 33 🕐 Lunch and dinner. Closed Tue and Jan

EL MOSQUI (€€)

Housed in a building resembling an upturned boat and noted for its rice and fish; busy at weekends.

✉ Subida al Faro 50 ☎ 968 56 45 63 🕐 Lunch and dinner, weekends only in low season

CARAVACA DE LA CRUZ

LOS VIÑALES (€)

Inland Murcian cooking. Excellent meat dishes, good vegetables and cheese tart for pudding. Local wines only.

✉ Avenida Juan Carlos I 41 ☎ 968 70 84 58 🕐 Lunch and dinner. Closed Tue and for two weeks in Oct

CARTAGENA

MARE NOSTRUM (€€)

Low-key but elegant restaurant with great sea views. Local dishes.

✉ Puerto Alfonso XII, Puerto Deportivo ☎ 968 52 21 31 🕐 Lunch and dinner

JUMILLA

MONASTERIO (€)

A large restaurant on the outskirts of town; a

Spanish experience.

✉ Avenida de la Asunción 40 ☎ 968 78 20 92 🕐 Lunch and dinner. Closed Tue

LA MANGA DEL MAR MENOR

AMAPOLA (€€€)

Open to non-residents, the Hyatt Club's elegant restaurant serves local ingredients with an international twist.

✉ Hyatt La Manga Club Resort, Los Belones ☎ 968 33 12 34 🕐 Lunch and dinner

BORSALINO (€€)

If you feel like a change from Spanish dishes this is a good place to eat. French dishes appear alongside local specialities such as fish baked in salt.

✉ Edificio Babylonia ☎ 968 56 31 30 🕐 Lunch and dinner. Closed Tue in winter and 7 Jan–12 Feb

MULA

VENTA LA MAGDALENA (€)

First-rate upcountry cooking using the freshest ingredients in simple surroundings. Excellent rabbit and rice dishes; house wine.

✉ Baños de Mula ☎ 968 66 05 68 🕐 Lunch and dinner. Closed on Wed and 15 Jul–15 Aug

PUERTO DE MAZARRÓN

VIRGEN DEL MAR (€)

Agreeable local restaurant with a friendly, relaxed atmosphere. Try the shellfish or fish dishes.

✉ Paseo Marítimo s/n ☎ 968 59 50 57 🕐 Lunch only

HEALTHY EATING

On a Spanish holiday it's not just the sun and relaxation that does you good, it's also what you eat. A traditional Spanish diet is not only delicious but healthy. Good bread, olive oil, fish, large quantities of fresh fruit and vegetables are the staples, with meat, dairy produce and sweet things in just the right quantity. Spaniards drink little alcohol and lots of water, ideal in the high summer temperatures.

Around Alicante

PRICES

Prices are approximate, based on a double room in high season, excluding breakfast and IVA, the Spanish equivalent of VAT.

€ = under €35
€€ = €35–€70
€€€= over €70

HOTEL GRADINGS

Officially registered hotels in Spain range from one to five stars (with an additional top de luxe category of GL, Gran Lujo). Other types of accommodation include apartment hotels, hotel residences (no restaurant), hostels and pensions. Stars are assigned according to service and facilities. Suites can usually be found in the four- or five-star range. Tariffs should be displayed by law.

ALICANTE (ALACANT)

ALMIRANTE (€€)

On the seafront at San Juan, this is an ideal choice for watersports enthusiasts. Friendly staff and a good restaurant.
✉ Avenida Niza 38 ☎ 965 65 01 12; www.hotelalmirante.com

CASTILLA ALICANTE (€€)

Comfortable, modern, well-equipped hotel, one block back from the beach at San Juan. Good-sized rooms all with balcony. Pool, shady palms and full bar and restaurant service.
✉ Avenida Países Escandinavos 7 ☎ 965 16 20 33; www.hcastilla.com

COVADONGA (€€)

A good central air-conditioned choice with parking and a garage. Ask for one of the quieter interior rooms.
✉ Plaza de los Luceros 17 ☎ 965 20 28 44

MEDITERRÁNEA PLAZA (€€€)

Stylish, comfortable hotel in the centre of the old town, facing the Ayuntamiento and a stone's throw from the sea.
✉ Pl de Ayuntamiento 6 ☎ 965 21 01 88; www.hotelmediterraneaplaza.com

LES MONGES (€€)

This friendly, family-run hotel is in a turn-of-the-19th-century building with attractive quirkily decorated rooms, right in the centre of town.
✉ Monges 2–1 ☎ 965 21 50 46

RAMBLA 9 (€€)

Centrally situated budget hotel with nice rooms and air-conditioning, on a wide avenue leading to the sea.
✉ Rambla Méndez Núñez 9 ☎ 965 14 45 80; www.hotelrambla.com

SIDI SAN JUAN (€€€)

The ultimate in resort hotels a little north of the city centre. Lovely views, every comfort, three pools and access to the beach via manicured grounds.
✉ La Doblada s/n, Playa de San Juan ☎ 965 16 13 00; www.hotelsidi.es

ALCOY (ALCOI)

MAS DE PAU (€€)

This beautifully restored 18th-century granary is in lovely countryside 9km east of Alcoy with superb views. Rather small rooms, but worth it for the pool, restaurant and ambience.
✉ Carretera Alcoy-Penáguila, km 9 ☎ 965 51 31 09

BIAR

VILLA DE BIAR (€€)

Delightful hotel, with elegant public rooms and lovely views. It incorporates the palace of the viscounts of Valdesoto.
✉ San José 2 ☎ 965 81 13 04; www.fanecaes-alicante.com

ELCHE (ELX)

CANDELIJAS (€€)

A good, family-run budget hotel in the centre of town. Clean, well-equipped rooms, all with bathrooms and air-conditioning.
✉ Doctor Ferrán 19 ☎ 965 46 65 12

HUERTO DEL CURA (€€€)

A luxurious hotel, affiliated to the state *paradors*, opposite the famous garden. Lovely grounds, every facility and an excellent restaurant.

🖂 Porta de la Morera 14
☎ 966 61 00 11;
www.huertodelcura.com

GUARDAMAR

EDÉN MAR (€€)

Summer season, excellent budget hotel. Near the beach.

🖂 Avenida Mediterráneo 19
☎ 965 72 92 13

MERIDIONAL (€€€)

Pleasant holiday hotel, on the beach. No pool, but tennis and friendly staff.

🖂 Urbanización Dunas de Guardamar ☎ 965 72 83 40;
www.hotelmeridional.es

ORIHUELA

SH PALACIO DE TUDEMIR (€€€)

Lovely hotel in a beautifully restored 18th-century palace in the historic heart of Orihuela. Facilities and service in keeping with a hotel of this calibre.

🖂 Alfonso XIII 1
☎ 965 73 80 10; e-mail: palaciotudemir@sh-serotel.com

SANTA POLA

MARINA PALACE (€€)

Modern hotel, with pool, large rooms and excellent restaurant, ten minutes from Alicante airport.

🖂 Carretera Alicante-Cartagena km 17 ☎ 965 41 13 12;
www.hotelmarinapalace.com

POLAMAR (€€€)

Large seafront hotel next to the port and sailing club. Popular with Spanish families; good restaurant and views.

🖂 Playa de Levante 6
☎ 965 41 32 00;
e-mail: info@polamar.com

TABARCA

CASA DEL GOBERNADOR (€€)

A wonderful hotel in the 18th-century governor's house in Tabarca.

🖂 Azhar 20 s/n, Isla de Tabarca
☎ 965 96 08 86;
www.casadelgobernador.com

TORREVIEJA

LLOYDS CLUB (€€€)

An apartment hotel with a restaurant and pool in a superb beach-side position. Well-equipped apartments, each with its own kitchen and a terrace overlooking the sea.

🖂 Avenida de los Holandeses 2
☎ 966 92 00 00

MASA INTERNACIONAL (€€€)

A comfortable hotel on a promontory overlooking the sea, a little outside town.

🖂 Avenida Alfredo Nobel 150
☎ 966 92 15 37; e-mail: hotel-masa@arrakis.es

VILLENA

SALVADORA (€€)

An old-fashioned hotel, with better facilities than its one-star rating would imply. Good restaurant.

🖂 Avenida de la Constitución 102 ☎ 965 80 09 50;
www.hotelsalvadora.com

VALUE FOR MONEY

Many visitors to the Costa Blanca stay in beach hotels in the main resorts. Taken as part of a package tour, such accommodation offers excellent value for money. But seaside hotels tend to be expensive when booked independently. Remember that inland hotels are generally much cheaper and will often give you a more authentic Spanish experience. Whether or not you hire a car, a night away won't wreck the holiday budget and will give you a chance to explore further from base.

Benidorm & the North

TRAVELLERS WITH DISABILITIES

Facilities for travellers with disabilities are gradually improving on the Costa Blanca, though progress is far from fast. An increasing number of hotels do have good access for wheelchairs, wide lifts and doorways, and easy parking, though ground-floor rooms are few and far between. Blue Flag beaches have ramps down to the beach, but getting around inland villages is not always easy. If you have special needs contact your tour operator or the hotel in advance. For further information contact: Federacio Ecom ✉ Gran Via de les Corts Catalanes 562, 08011 Barcelona ☎ 934 51 55 50; www.ecom.es

BENIDORM

AGIR (€€€)
A long-established hotel on Benidorm's main avenue.
✉ Avenida Mediterráneo 11 ☎ 965 85 51 62; www.hotelagir.com

BRISTOL PARK (€€€)
In a traditional-style building, fairly small, but offering the full range of services, including a pool.
✉ C/ Doctor Fleming ☎ 965 85 14 482; www.onasol.es

CLIMBEL (€€€)
One of Benidorm's most traditional hotels, next to the Playa de Levante, with a pool and air-conditioning.
✉ Avenida Europa 1 ☎ 965 85 21 00; www.hotelclimbel.com

FLEMING (€€)
Good-value, typically Spanish family-run hotel, near both the beach and town centre, with a pool and garden.
✉ Maravall 11 ☎ 965 85 32 62

GRAN HOTEL DELFÍN (€€€)
At the far end of the Playa de Poniente in an oasis of sub-tropical gardens, with good service and clean rooms. (Closed Nov to mid-March.)
✉ Av Mont Benidorm 13 ☎ 965 85 34 00; www.granhoteldelfin.com

SOL PELICANOS OCAS (€€€)
Four pools, tennis courts and close to beach; ideal for families looking for style and comfort. All rooms have balconies. Entertainment for all ages.
✉ Gerona 45–47 ☎ 965 85 23 50; www.solmelia.com

ALTEA

ALATAYA (€€€)
Long-established hotel renovated in 2000, over-looking the seaside *paseo*. Big, comfortable rooms with sea views, and with a good restaurant.
✉ Sant Pere 28 ☎ 965 84 08 00; www.hotelaltea.com

CALPE (CALP)

GALETAMAR (€€)
Modern, well-equipped hotel with balconies, sea views, good-size pool and spacious lounge areas. Accommodation includes family rooms and individual bungalows.
✉ La Caleta 28 ☎ 965 83 23 11; www.galetamar.com

VENTA LA CHATA (€€)
A family-run hotel in a 200-year-old country house in the countryside between Calpe and Benissa, with views to the mountains and the sea.
✉ Carretera N-332 km 172 ☎ 965 83 03 08

COCENTAINA

ELS FRARES (€€)
A tiny hotel well outside the town in an elegantly restored old house, in a mountain village with wonderful views. Peaceful and quiet, a warm welcome and interesting cooking.
✉ Avenida del País Valencia, Quatretondeta ☎ 965 51 12 34; www.mountainwalks.com

DÉNIA

LOS ANGELES (€€)
A pleasant resort hotel with direct access to the beach, a little north of Dénia in the busy Les Marines area.
✉ Playa de Les Marines km 4 ☎ 965 78 04 58; www.hotel losangelesdenia.com

BUENAVISTA (€€€)
Surrounded by pine trees, this small and lovely hotel, with a pool, is in a skilfully converted 19th-century mansion. The restaurant accents local dishes.
✉ Partida Tossalet 82 ☎ 965 78 79 95; www.hotel-buenavista.com

GANDÍA

BAYREN 1 (€€)
A classic seaside hotel right on the beachfront, with all facilities.
✉ Paseo Neptuno 62 ☎ 962 84 03 00; www.hotelesbayren.com

BORGIA (€€)
A hotel not aimed purely at holidaymakers, near the town centre, with good-sized rooms.
✉ República Argentina 5 ☎ 962 87 81 09; www.hghotels.com

GUADALEST

EL TRESTELLADOR (€)
A small family-run mountain hotel high in the Guadalest valley. Simple comfortable rooms, fine views and excellent local cooking.
✉ Partida del Trestellador, Benimantell ☎ 965 88 52 21; e-mail: eltrestellador@netvision.es

JÁTIVA (XÀTIVA)

HOSTERÍA DE MONT SANT (€€€)
An elegant and historic country house hotel on the hillside above the town and below the castle. Lovely gardens, pool and superb views.
✉ Carretera del Castillo s/n ☎ 962 27 50 81; www.montsac.com

JÁVEA (XÀBIA)

PARADOR DE JÁVEA (€€€)
The only *parador* on the Costa Blanca, the de Jávea is a modern, luxury hotel in verdant gardens. There is direct beach access and a high level of service.
✉ Mediterráneo 7 ☎ 965 70 93 08; www.parador.es

MORAIRA

SWISS MORAIRA (€€€)
A relatively small hotel, the Swiss Moraira is set back from the sea in a beautiful valley and offers comfort and tranquillity. With pool and tennis court.
✉ Haya 175, Urbanizacion Club Moraira ☎ 965 74 71 04

VILLAJOYOSA (LA VILA JOIOSA)

EL MONTÍBOLI (€€€)
Justifiably described in its publicity material as 'a corner of paradise', this luxury hotel is on a promontory above two secluded bays and backed by hills. It is also known for its superb restaurants.
✉ Partida Montiboli s/n ☎ 965 89 02 50; www.elmontiboli.com

SELF-CATERING

Renting a villa or flat, whether it's on the coast or in some tranquil rural backwater, gives you much more freedom of choice than an 'all-inclusive' stay. Then there's the added pleasure of trying different bars and restaurants for dinner, or shopping at the market and cooking something good at home. You can book such accommodation as part of a flight-inclusive holiday, or directly through the owners and their agents. Local tourist offices have lists of self-catering options available by post or fax.

Murcia

LIVING LIKE THE SPANISH

If you decide to tour around and stay in inland towns and villages, you may find things a little different from the international standards of the coast. Modest country hotels will tend to have showers rather than baths and no air-conditioning, so keep the shutters closed during the heat of the day. Eating is more geared to local habits, so lunch and dinner are late.

MURCIA

ARCO DE SAN JUAN (€€€)

One of the city's great hotels, in Murcia's historic centre. Tasteful and comfortable, hidden behind an 18th-century façade, with friendly and professional service.
✉ Plaza Ceballos 10 ☎ 968 21 04 55; www.arcosanjuan.com

CASA EMILIO (€€)

A good budget choice with clean and comfortable rooms, this small hotel lies across the river within 10 minutes' walk of the historic centre.
✉ Alameda de Colón 9 ☎ 968 22 06 31

DESVÍO-RINCÓN DE PACO (€)

Friendly owner, basic rooms and good location – near the bus station.
✉ Cortés 27 ☎ 968 21 84 36

HISPANO II (€€)

A traditional Murcian hotel, in the centre, with good service and comfortable rooms.
✉ Radio Murcia 3 ☎ 968 21 61 52; www.ono.com/hotelhispano

ÁGUILAS

AL SUR (€€€)

It's worth driving out of Aguilas to reach this Mediterranean-style hotel, on a promontory with great sea views, friendly proprietors and a laid-back atmosphere.
✉ Torre de Copa 24, Calabardina ☎ 968 41 94 66

CARLOS III (€€)

A small hotel in the bustling centre of town, professionally and courteously run, with comfortable rooms.
✉ Avenida Carlos III 22 ☎ 968 41 16 50; www.hotelcarlosiii.com

CARAVACA DE LA CRUZ

CENTRAL (€€)

A good base for exploring the Segura valley, this small country town hotel, with comfortable rooms and friendly service, gives a taste of inland Spain.
✉ Gran Via 18 ☎ 968 70 70 55

EL MOLINO DEL RÍO (€€)

A converted 16th-century mill in a truly rural setting in the undiscovered hinterland, high in the Argos valley system. Self-catering and hotel-type accommodation. The mill has a restaurant and pool.
✉ Camoni Viejo de Archivel ☎ 606 30 14 09; www.molinodelrio.com

CARTAGENA

ALFONSO XIII (€€€)

Cartagena's main central hotel, a large classical building with spacious rooms and elegant architecture.
✉ Paseo Alfonso XIII 40 ☎ 968 52 00 00; www.hotelalfonsoxiii.com

LOS HABANEROS (€€)

A good place to stay on the outskirts of the city, with parking. Known for its restaurant.
✉ San Diego 60 ☎ 968 50 52 50

FORTUNA

BALNEARIO (€€)
A wonderful Edwardian spa hotel with sweeping staircases and lofty public rooms. The pool is fed by the hot springs and the hotel basement contains the treatment rooms.
✉ Balneario s/n ☎ 968 68 50 11; www.leana.es

LA MANGA DEL MAR MENOR

LA CAVANNA (€€€)
This vast hotel, overlooking the Mar Menor, has every conceivable facility for holidaymakers and is a short walk from all the attractions.
✉ Plaza Cavanna s/n ☎ 968 56 36 00; www.entramares.com

DOS MARES (€€)
A small hotel right in the middle of the action. Clean and functional, it is excellent value for money.
✉ Plaza Bohemia s/n ☎ 968 14 00 93

HYATT REGENCY LA MANGA (€€€)
Murcia's only five-star hotel, with its own golf course. Superb service, along with an excellent restaurant, tennis facilities and a pool.
✉ Los Belones ☎ 968 33 12 34; www.lamanga.hyatt.com

SOL GALÚA (€€€)
This modern resort hotel, near the sea, offers big, comfortable rooms and all facilities, including 24-hour room service
✉ Hacienda Dos Mares ☎ 968 56 32 00; www.solmelia.com

VILLAS LA MANGA (€€)
A well-run hotel in the heart of the resort's strip of development, with excellent service and a pool.
✉ Gran Viá de la Manga s/n ☎ 968 14 52 22; www.villaslamanga.es

PUERTO DE MAZARRÓN

BAHÍA (€€)
A medium-sized hotel on the seafront. Simple décor and friendly staff.
✉ Playa de la Reya s/n ☎ 968 59 40 00; www.hotelbahia.com

LA CUMBRE (€€)
Truly a hotel with a view; conventional, comfortable rooms, friendly staff and acceptable food.
✉ Urbanización La Cumbre ☎ 968 59 48 61

MULA

ALCÁZAR (€)
Ideal if you're touring the inland sierras; this quintessentially Spanish hotel has rather small rooms of great charm.
✉ Carretera Pliego s/n ☎ 968 66 21 05

SAN PEDRO DEL PINATAR

TRAINA (€€)
Between the Mar Menor and the Mediterranean, this is a relaxing base for exploring the coast and adjacent salt flats. Has rooms for people with disabilities.
✉ Av Generalisimo 84, Lo Pagán ☎ 968 33 50 22; www.hoteltraina.com

SPAS

Murcia is well endowed with natural hot springs, whose waters relieve the discomfort of everything from arthritis to eczema. Most of them were used by the Romans and the Moors and they are still very popular. Spa hotels range from the incredibly luxurious, with beauty farms attached, to those emphasising treatments. Often in out-of-the-way places, they can make a peaceful base for exploring the inland areas, with the added bonus of a hot thermal swimming pool to ease away your aches and pains (► 60, Fortuna).

Arts, Crafts and Gifts

POTTERY IN TOTANA

The town of Totana is known for its pottery, made here since Moorish times. More than 20 potteries still function, producing an incredible range of ceramics, huge earthenware storage jars, pots and bowls. Some of these are still fired in the traditional Arab-style kiln, the *tosta*, where the pots stand on a perforated floor above the heat source. Workshops still produce the *cántara de Totana*, a traditional pitcher, probably first designed by the Romans. If you're shopping, head for the old pottery district in town, rather than the outlets aimed at the tourists along the main road. Totana is quickly reached down the motorway from Murcia and lies on the edge of Murcia's splendid sierras.

CENTROS DE ARTESANÍA

Murcia is justly proud of the range and quality of hand-produced crafts made within its borders, which range from pottery and woodwork to fabrics and embroidery. The regional government has set up centres in several major towns specifically to help the artisans involved by showing and selling their work under one roof. Here, interested visitors can see the full range of local crafts, buy anything that appeals to them, or be advised on where to find something specific. These centres are well worth a visit and you can find them in Murcia, Cartagena and Lorca.

ALFARERÍA BELLÓN

A specialist ceramicist, making modern pots using shapes, techniques and colours reminiscent of the earliest Iberian ware.
✉ Paseo Ollería 19, Totana
☎ 968 42 48 01

ARTESANIA

An interesting shop carrying a large, attractive range of ceramics, pottery and other crafts from the Alicante region.
✉ V Pascual Alfonso X el Sabio 15, Alicante ☎ 965 14 01 39

ARTESANÍA ABELLÁN

A wonderful shop specialising in handmade Belén figures, the traditional miniatures used in Christmas cribs.
✉ Mayor 16, Bo del Progreso, Murcia ☎ 968 25 28 06

CENTRO REGIONAL DE ARTESANÍA

Half-shop, half-exhibition, with the whole range of traditional Murcian handicrafts, and information on where you can find the actual craftsmen.
✉ Francisco Rabal 8, Murcia
☎ 968 28 45 85 🕔 Mon–Fri 11–2, 4:30–7:30, Sat 11–2

CERAMICA LES SORTS

Colourful pottery from all over Valencia is piled high in this crammed shop.
✉ Edif Kristal Mar 18D–18E, Moraira ☎ 965 74 57 37

CERÁMICAS ARTESANAS

You'll discover plenty of colourful ceramics at this tiny shop.
✉ Sánchez Moya, Benidorm
☎ 965 85 73 47

CERÁMICAS VALLES

You could spend hours pottering around this big showroom, which sells vibrant, hand-painted ceramics and pottery from all over Spain, as well as leather, garden pots and rather dubious paintings.
✉ Urb Los Piños D-5, Ctra Calpe-Moraira Km 2, Calpe
☎ 965 833 661

EL POVEO

A well-known outlet for one of Totana's major ceramic producers, with pots and other products beautifully made..
✉ Rambla s/n, Totana
☎ 968 42 19 52

LOLA MIR

Lots of arty-crafty decor items for the house.
✉ Emilio Delgado 4, Altea
☎ 965 84 05 88

MERCADILLO DE VERANO

A daily summer market with a fascinating mix of stalls selling traditional and modern crafts.
✉ Esplanada de Cervantes, Dénia ☎ None

SILK

An Aladdin's cave of gifts with a difference, that specialises in handmade crafts and textiles from India, China and Nepal.
✉ C/ Médico Pascual Pérez 13, Alicante ☎ 965 20 85 91

YELMO ANTIGÜEDADES

One of the best antique shops in the Costa Blanca region, but the prices are a bit on the high side.
✉ Sagasta 34 and 42, Cartagena ☎ 968 52 54 13

Fashion, Leather and Jewellery

AMOR AMOR

Clothes shop for women with a wide range of designs for many occasions.

✉ Avenida Martinez Alejos 3, Benidorm ☎ 965 85 13 95

BERNARDINO

Shoes from this Elche-based manufacturer.

✉ San Miguel 16, Elche
☎ 965 45 21 93;
✉ Diagonal 5, Elche
☎ 965 43 63 89

BOLSOS PACO

Deliciously soft bags, travel goods, belts, wallets and purses.

✉ Patricio Ferrandiz 27, Dénia
☎ 966 42 13 12

BOTTICELLI

Exquisite leather handbags and shoes; one of a chain of three in town.

✉ Gran Via s/n, Alicante
☎ 965 24 01 65

BOUTIQUE BOLÉ BOLÉ

Classic and not-so-classic designs of ladies' clothes.

✉ Plaza Ruperto Chapí 6, Alicante ☎ 965 14 30 33

CHARRO

Eco-friendly men's fashion in natural fabrics with laid-back styles and low prices.

✉ Calle Santa Fax 4, Benidorm
☎ None

GOYA ORO

Upmarket jeweller.

✉ Martínez Alejos 3, Benidorm
☎ 966 83 10 50

JACADI

This stylish shop has a range of children's clothes.

✉ Teatro 46, Alicante
☎ 965 14 35 45

JOYERÍA GÓMEZ

An upmarket jeweller with some attractive and typically Spanish designs.

✉ Corredora 6, Elche
☎ 965 45 28 50

MERCA PIEL

The place to come for a leather coat with a good choice and price range.

✉ Paseo de la Carretera 20, Benidorm ☎ 965 85 02 56

PECAS CALZADOS

A popular shoe shop with a range of styles at very good prices.

✉ La Cruz 6, Gandia ☎ 962 87 73 16; ✉ Mayor 60, Gandia ☎ 962 87 69 44

RITUAL

Pure cotton and silk skirts, trousers, shirts and dresses from India and the Far East.

✉ Marques de Campo 26, Dénia
☎ 966 43 01 19

SALVADOR ARTESANO

Out-of-town factory outlet for one of Elche's main shoe and leather manufacturers. Look out for some amazing bargains.

✉ Carretera Murcia–Alicante km 45, Elche ☎ 966 67 54 41

SAQUETA

Soft leather bags, purses and wallets.

✉ Mayor 17, Gandia
☎ 962 87 97 92

YACARÉ

This exquisite leather shop is one of Benidorm's few truly elegant stores. Classic bags, belts, purses and understated leather clothes.

✉ Avda Mediterráneo 14, Benidorm ☎ 966 80 54 06

WHERE TO SHOP

For serious shopping, the main towns of Alicante and Murcia have a good range of shops of all sorts. Gandía also prides itself on its facilities, with several shopping areas and markets for food and crafts. Leather goods are usually a good buy in this part of Spain, with soft and well-designed shoes top of the list.

CENTROS COMMERCIALES AND DEPARTMENT STORES

Most visitors to Spain enjoy shopping in the vast hypermarkets, which offer a huge range of food, drink, hardware and clothes. *Continente* is one of the best chains, with branches at Alicante, Benidorm, Elche, Oliva and Murcia. The nationwide chain of *El Corte Inglés*, founded in 1939 to sell English fabrics, has good general department stores. There are branches at Alicante and Murcia.

77

Food

MARKETS

There are two main types of market in Spain: the *mercado municipal*, a daily food market, and the *mercadillos*, weekly street markets. Food markets are held in the heart of town, and have stalls selling fruit and vegetables, meat, fish, dairy products, bread and pastries and flowers. They are colourful and fascinating, the prices are controlled and they are good places to put together a picnic. Street markets, on a specific day each week in all sizeable towns, are mostly devoted to clothes, shoes and household goods. They are fun to wander round and you can often pick up a bargain, but don't expect high style or quality. Tourist offices have details of their opening times and also of the huge Sunday-morning *mercadillos artesanos* (craft markets) held in various towns.

CONVENTO DE LA TRINIDAD

Spanish nuns maintain the old tradition of cake, sweet and pastry-making, using local recipes and the finest ingredients. You'll find traditional delicacies from Orihuela. Give your order and the goodies will appear on a turn-table.

✉ Convento de la Trinidad, C/ Overía 1, Orihuela
☎ None

COOPERATIVA AGRÍCOLA

Olive-oil enthusiasts can buy the best of the local oils straight from source here. Sizes range from 0.5 litre bottles to 5-litre cans.

✉ Mossén Eugeni Raduan 6, Cocentaina
☎ 965 59 02 67

DAMAS

A wonderful bar and *pastelería*, with a huge range of mouth-watering sweet and savoury creations.

✉ Pintor Lorenzo Casanova 5, Alicante ☎ 965 12 14 71

ESPECIALITIES LLORET

This upmarket food shop is a real boon for self-caterers. Also a good range of tempting edible souvenirs.

✉ Juan Carlos I-3, Villajoyosa (La Vila Joiosa)
☎ 965 89 03 93

ESPÍ

Stock up on *turrón* at this old-fashioned speciality shop in the centre.

✉ Lopéz Torregrosa 17, Alicante
☎ 965 21 44 41

EL TÚNEL

A good place to track down the traditional pastries and sweetmeats of Alcoy.

✉ San Lorenzo 34, Alcoy (Alcoi)
☎ 965 54 52 54

FONDA NEGRA

Old-established shop with a large range of high-quality Murcian foodstuffs.

✉ González Adalid 1, Murcia
☎ 968 21 15 63

L'ALTEANA

Sumptuous calorie-heavy bread and cakes as well as an interesting range of savoury mouthfuls.

✉ Avenida de la Nucia 13, Altea
☎ 965 84 03 07

PASTELERÍA CARLOS

A mecca for the sweet-toothed with cakes, pastries and traditional sweetmeats that are beautiful to look at and delicious to eat.

✉ Jaime el Conquistador 7, Murcia ☎ 968 23 30 20

PRALINES SOEN

A mecca for chocaholics with a wide range of Spanish and Belgian chocolates.

✉ Calle Gambo 2, Calpe
☎ 966 80 73 94; ✉ Avenida Gabriel Miró 41, Calpe
☎ 965 83 59 59

SANCT BERNHARD

An interesting herbalist, worth visiting for its wide range of products, including teas, creams and cleansers.

✉ Avenida Gabriel Miró 7, Calpe (Calp) ☎ 965 83 68 07

Miscellaneous

WINE

BODEGA CO-OPERATIVA SAN ISIDRO

Choose from a range of Jumilla *denominación de origen* wines.

✉ Carretera Murcia 32, Jumilla
☎ 968 78 07 00

BODEGA SELECCIÓN

An attractive wineshop well-stocked with over 400 different Spanish wines, *cavas* and liqueurs. There is also a selection of imported specialities.

✉ Avenida Constitución 22A, Orihuela
☎ 965 81 37 81

LA BOUTIQUE DEL VINO

A wide range of Spanish and foreign wines, spirits and liqueurs. It's a good place to find that special bottle to take home.

✉ Avda Atmella de Mar s/n, Benidorm
☎ 966 80 32 09

ENACOTECA BERNADINO

This upmarket wine merchant offers a huge range of Spanish vintages – there are more than 2,500 in total. The speciality is Rioja.

✉ C/ Alberola 38, Alicante
☎ 965 28 08 73

BOOKS & STATIONERY

BOUTIQUE DE LA PRENSA

A good newspaper and magazine outlet with a large range of papers and periodicals from all over Europe.

✉ Passeig de la Carretera 4, Benidorm ☎ 965 85 03 07

EX LIBRIS

This well-stocked bookstore has lovely photographic and art books, as well as an excellent selection of locally themed guide and picture books and maps. They also carry both Spanish and foreign magazines.

✉ Plaza Jorge Juan 7, Dénia
☎ 966 43 15 52

LIBRERÍA INTERNACIONAL

An excellent and wide-ranging bookshop, with helpful staff, specialising in maps and charts.

✉ Rafael Altamira 6, Alicante
☎ 965 21 79 25

LIBROS ESCUDERO

Second-hand bookshop with a huge selection of English paperbacks, as well as old postcards, posters and cigarette cards.

✉ Santa Faz 47, Benidorm
☎ 650 57 55 20

BEAUTY PRODUCTS

PERFUMERIA BERNABEU

These sister stores carry a large range of makes and types of skin-care products and scents.

✉ Mayor 42, Gandia ☎ 962 87 65 40
✉ San Francisco de Borja 52, Gandia ☎ 962 87 42 11

MONÓVAR

A visit to the thriving little town of Monóvar (Monòver) is a must for wine-lovers. The 19th century saw the strong, slightly sweet Monóvar reds fetching astronomical prices after phylloxera destroyed French vineyards. Production of the wine has continued into the 21st century, and wine-tasting is available at Bodega Salvador Poveda. Monóvar is 40km west of Alicante.

Cinema, Theatre & Concerts

BULLFIGHTING

Whatever your feelings about the ethics of this essentially Spanish experience, bullfighting is a fact of life here and every town of any size has a bullring. Fights take place on Sunday afternoons throughout the summer season and there are large rings in Alicante, Benidorm and Murcia, as well as some of the smaller towns.

Despite the large number of foreign residents, there is little foreign-language entertainment on the Costa Blanca. Benidorm has a number of floor shows and cabarets which need no translation, and cinemas in the main resorts occasionally feature foreign-language films. Alicante and Murcia have a lively Spanish arts scene; the tourist offices have details. Weekly newspapers are published in English, German and Dutch on the coast, with details of what's on where.

ALICANTE (ALACANT)

TEATRO PRINCIPAL
✉ Plaza Ruperto Chapí 7
☎ 965 20 23 80

ALTEA

LA PLAZA
Live jazz on Friday nights.
✉ Plaza de la Inglesia
☎ None

PALAU ALTEA
Altea's millennium arts centre offers music, theatre and dance.
✉ Palau Altea, Casc Antic
☎ 902 33 22 11

ELCHE (ELX)

GRAN TEATRO
Theatre, classical music and films in Spanish.
✉ Hospital 26 ☎ 965 45 14 03

ORIHUELA

TEATRO CIRCO
Concerts, theatre and shows for Spanish-speakers, in a beautifully restored turn-of-the-19th-century circular theatre.
✉ Ronda de Santo Domingo
☎ 966 74 01 04

BENIDORM

BENIDORM PALACE
Very popular international floor show and cabaret with optional dinner.
✉ Avenida Dr Severo Ochoa s/n
☎ 965 85 16 60

CASTILLO FORTALEZA DE ALFAZ
Enjoy a mock medieval banquet, then experience a visit to the chamber of horrors.
✉ Carretera Benidorm–Albir
☎ 966 86 55 92

EL CENTRO CINEMA
✉ Murcia s/n ☎ 965 85 83 12

MOLINO BENIDORM
An amusing floor show, followed by a male striptease.
✉ Avenida Beniardá 2
☎ 966 80 23 08

GATA DE GORGOS

EUROPA CINEMA
English-language films are shown at this cinema on Tuesdays.
✉ Escolar 14
☎ 965 75 62 62

MURCIA

TEATRO ROMEA
A full programme of Spanish plays and concerts is staged in this handsome 19th-century theatre.
✉ Plaza Julián Romea 7
☎ 968 21 16 11

Casinos, Bars & Nightclubs

CASINOS

Dress is normally smart-casual. You must be over 18 to enter. Remember to take your passport.

VILLAJOYOSA (LA VILA JOIOSA)

CASINO COSTA BLANCA
✉ Carretera Alicante–Valencia km 141.5 ☎ 965 89 07 00
🕓 8PM–4AM (5AM Fri, Sat)

CARTAGENA

CASINO CARTAGENA
✉ Mayor 17 ☎ 968 50 10 10
🕓 10–2, 5–11

MURCIA

GRAN CASINO MURCIA
✉ Apostoles 34 ☎ 968 21 23 08 🕓 6PM–4AM

LA MANGA

CASINO DEL MAR MENOR
✉ Gran Via La Manga s/n
☎ 968 14 06 04 🕓 Sun–Thu 9PM–4AM, Fri, Sat 9PM–5AM

BARS & NIGHTCLUBS

ALICANTE (ALACANT)

EL CARIBE
A hip-swinging Latino club with salsa and *merengue*.
✉ Calle General Primo de Riera 14 ☎ None 🕓 Tue–Thu 8:30PM–4AM, Fri–Sat 10:30PM–4:30AM

PACHA
Lively disco on one of the town's main streets.
✉ Avenida de Aguilera 38
☎ None 🕓 11PM–6AM

BENIDORM

KM
KM has a reputation for its music, terraces and beautiful people.
✉ Antigua Ctra N-332
☎ None 🕓 11PM–6AM, Easter–Oct

PENELOPE
A huge, noisy and sophisticated disco, popular with Benidorm regulars for years.
✉ Antigua Ctra N-322
☎ None 🕓 11PM–6AM

DÉNIA

IMPERIAL
Just outside town on the main Jávea road.
✉ Carretera Jávea ☎ None
🕓 10:30PM–5AM, Easter–Oct

LA MANGA

ZEPPELIN
One of the liveliest disco bars along La Manga's main boulevard, with the action starting late and continuing often until after dawn.
✉ Gran Via de la Manga
☎ None 🕓 11PM–6AM

MURCIA

DISCOTECA THE NIGHT CLUB
Starts to hum after 1AM when most people arrive.
✉ Puerta Nueva ☎ None
🕓 11:30PM–6AM, Thu–Sat

SANTA POLA

DISCOTECA CAMELOT
People drive miles to this disco.
✉ Gran Playa ☎ None
🕓 11PM–6AM

NIGHTLIFE

The Costa Blanca has an animated night scene and the streets in some resorts are busy until the early hours of the morning. Benidorm has numerous discos and clubs and an eclectic range of music. The club to be seen at varies from year to year and word of mouth should lead you in the right direction. Many popular clubs are situated in huge buildings outside towns, usually just a taxi hop away. Many bars have live music with jazz, easy listening and even the occasional burst of flamenco on offer. The larger hotels often have after-dinner dancing. Opening times are flexible, but the action starts very late, often after midnight, and carries on till around dawn. Prices vary, with some clubs charging a hefty entrance fee, which usually includes one free drink.

81

Sport

SPORT

The main emphasis is on outdoor and water-based sports. Sailing and scuba-diving are popular, with excellent facilities in the major resorts, while golf courses have multiplied. Cyclists and walkers will find great opportunities in the hills behind the coast. Most places have tennis courts and larger centres offer a good programme of spectator sports, from football and rugby to athletics.

GOLF

The Costa Blanca area has more than 20 prestigious and beautifully laid-out golf courses, as well as some smaller ones, and the game brings many visitors to the region. Golf package holidays are increasingly popular. Most courses have clubs and trolleys or buggies for hire and a full range of ancillary services, such as practice ranges, pro shops and club houses. You may be asked for a handicap certificate and you should book in advance as courses can be very busy.

BOWLING

BENIDORM

BOWLING CENTRE BENIDORM
✉ Avenida Mediterráneo 22
☎ 965 85 41 87

BOWLING GREEN BENIDORM
✉ Partida Almafrá s/n
☎ 965 85 77 43

GOLF

ALICANTE

CLUB DE GOLF ALENDA
✉ Autovía Alicante–Madrid km 15 ☎ 965 62 05 21

CALPE (CALP)

CLUB DE GOLF DON CAYO
✉ Urbanización El Aramo–Sierra de Altea
☎ 965 84 80 46

DÉNIA

CLUB DE GOLF LA SELLA
✉ Carretera La Xara–Jesús Pobre ☎ 966 45 42 52

JÁVEA (XÀBIA)

CLUB DE GOLF JÁVEA
✉ Carretera Jávea–Benitachell km 4.5 ☎ 965 79 25 84

LA MANGA

CLUB DE GOLF LOS BELONES
✉ La Manga Club Hyatt Complex ☎ 968 13 72 34

CLUB DE GOLF TORRE PACHECO
✉ Torre Pacheco
☎ 968 57 90 37

MORAIRA

CLUB DE GOLF IFACH
✉ Carretera Moraira–Calpe km 3, Urbanización San Jaime
☎ 966 49 71 14

ORIHUELA

CLUB DE GOLF VILLA MARTÍN
✉ Carretera Alicante– Cartagena km 50 ☎ 966 76 51 27

RIDING

ALICANTE

CLUB HÍPICO DE CAMPOAMOR
✉ Carretera Cartagena–Alicante km 48
☎ 965 32 13 66

DÉNIA

ESCUELA DE EQUITACIÓN LA SELLA
✉ Carretera La Xara–Jesús Pobre
☎ 965 76 14 55

LA MANGA

EL PUNTAL
✉ La Manga Club Hyatt, Los Belones
☎ 968 13 72 34

SAILING

ÁGUILAS

CLUB NÁUTICO ISLAS MENORES
✉ Puerto Marítima, Cartagena
☎ 968 13 33 55

ALICANTE

CLUB NÁUTICO COSTA BLANCA
✉ Avenida de la Condomina 20
☎ 965 15 44 91

Where to be Entertained

DÉNIA

CLUB NÁUTICO DÉNIA
✉ Carretera Dénia–Jávea 1
☎ 965 78 09 89

LA MANGA

SURF-PLAYA
✉ La Manga del Mar Menor
☎ 968 14 00 20

MAZARRÓN

CLUB NÁUTICO DE MAZARRÓN
✉ Cabezo de Cebada s/n
☎ 968 59 40 11

MORAIRA

ANTIPODES SAILING SCHOOL
✉ Puerto de Moraira
☎ 965 83 83 10

SANTA POLA

CLUB NÁUTICO DE SANTA POLA
✉ Muella de Poniente s/n
☎ 965 41 24 03

SCUBA DIVING

You can dive under supervision with one of the many diving clubs in the area. If you want to dive alone, bring your international proficiency certificate.

ÁGUILAS

LA ALMADRABA
✉ Ernest Hemingway 13, Calabardina
☎ 968 41 96 32

BENIDORM

CLUB POSEIDON
✉ Santander 9, Alfaz 4, Edif Silvia ☎ 965 85 32 27

SCUBA DIVING BENIDORM
✉ Avenida Otta de Habsburgo 10 ☎ 966 80 97 12

CABO DE PALOS

ISLAS HORMIGAS CLUB
✉ Cabo de Palos
☎ 968 14 55 30

CALPE (CALP)

ESPAÑA BAJOEL MAR
✉ Puerto Blanco
☎ 965 83 13 37

DÉNIA

AQUATIC DÉNIA
✉ Carretera Dénia–Jávea 3d, Les Rotes ☎ 966 42 52 15

MAZARRÓN

ZOEA MAZARRÓN
✉ Plaza del Mar 20
☎ 968 15 40 06

WATERSKIING

BENIDORM

CABLE SKI
✉ Racó de L'Oix, Playa de Levante ☎ 965 85 13 86

WINDSURFING

BENIDORM

ESCUELA DE WINDSURF WAIKIKI
✉ Playa de Levante
☎ 965 83 28 56

LA MANGA

MULTISPORTS CENTRE MAR MENOR
✉ La Manga del Mar Menor
☎ 968 57 00 21

WATERSPORTS

With its mild winter and long hot summers the coast provides ideal conditions for watersports practically year-round. Marina facilities are excellent everywhere. Inexperienced mariners will find sailing schools at all the main resorts with hire and tuition available. The sheltered Mar Menor is a particularly good spot for beginners. Windsurfing and waterskiing are also on offer. There are plenty of boat excursions up and down the Costa Blanca.

SWIMMING

Beaches (➤ 50–51) vary up and down the coast from shingle and pebbles to the finest sand. They often sport the Blue Flag award, which guarantees their cleanliness, safety and facilities. The main towns – Alicante, Benidorm and Murcia – all have heated indoor pools for winter swimming.

83

COSTA BLANCA
practical matters

WHAT YOU NEED

	UK	Germany	USA	Netherlands
● Required ○ Suggested ▲ Not required	Some countries require a passport to remain valid for a minimum period (usually at least six months) beyond the date of entry — contact the embassy or your travel agent for details.			
Passport (or National Identity Card where applicable)	●	●	●	●
Visa (regulations can change — check before booking your journey)	▲	▲	▲	▲
Onward or Return Ticket	▲	▲	●	▲
Health Inoculations	▲	▲	▲	▲
Health documentation (Health, ➤ 90)	●	●	●	●
Travel Insurance	○	○	○	○
Valid Driving Licence	●	●	●	●
Car Insurance Certificate	●	●	●	●
Car Registration Document	●	●	●	●

WHEN TO GO

Costa Blanca

■ High season

■ Low season

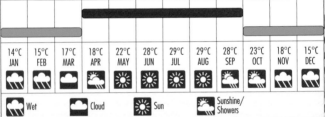

14°C JAN	15°C FEB	17°C MAR	18°C APR	22°C MAY	28°C JUN	29°C JUL	29°C AUG	28°C SEP	23°C OCT	18°C NOV	15°C DEC

Wet	Cloud	Sun	Sunshine/Showers

TIME DIFFERENCES

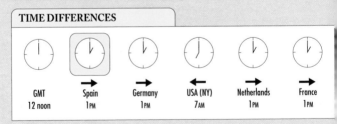

GMT 12 noon	Spain 1PM	Germany 1PM	USA (NY) 7AM	Netherlands 1PM	France 1PM

TOURIST OFFICES

In the UK
Spanish Tourist Office
79 New Cavendish Street
London W1W 6XB
☎ 020 7486 8077
email: londres@tourspain.es

In the USA
Tourist Office of Spain
666 Fifth Avenue
New York
NY 10103
☎ 212/265 8822
email: oetny@tourspain.es

In Canada
Spanish National Tourist Office
102 Bloor St W, 34th floor
Toronto, Ontario
M4W 3E2
☎ 416 961 3131

ARRIVING

Spain's national airline, Iberia (☎ 0990 341 341; www.iberia.com), has scheduled flights to Alicante's El Altet and Valencia's Manises airports from major Spanish and European cities.

El Altet Airport
Kilometres to Alicante city centre

10 kilometres

Journey times	
🚋	N/A
🚌	40 minutes
🚗	15 minutes

Manises Airport
Kilometres to Valencia city centre

15 kilometres

Journey times	
🚋	N/A
🚌	45 minutes
🚗	20 minutes

MONEY

The euro (€) is the official currency of Spain. Euro banknotes and coins were introduced in January 2002. Banknotes are issued in denominations of 5, 10, 20, 50, 100, 200 and 500 euros; coins in denominations of 1, 2, 5, 10, 20 and 50 cents, and 1 and 2 euros. Spain's former currency, the peseta, went out of circulation in February 2002.
Major credit cards are widely accepted. Some credit and debit cards can also be used to withdraw euro notes from ATMs.
You may have to pay a high commission to cash Euro traveller's cheques.

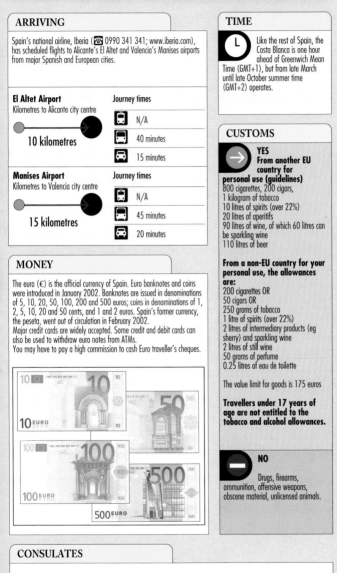

TIME

Like the rest of Spain, the Costa Blanca is one hour ahead of Greenwich Mean Time (GMT+1), but from late March until late October summer time (GMT+2) operates.

CUSTOMS

**YES
From another EU country for personal use (guidelines)**
800 cigarettes, 200 cigars,
1 kilogram of tobacco
10 litres of spirits (over 22%)
20 litres of aperitifs
90 litres of wine, of which 60 litres can be sparkling wine
110 litres of beer

From a non-EU country for your personal use, the allowances are:
200 cigarettes OR
50 cigars OR
250 grams of tobacco
1 litre of spirits (over 22%)
2 litres of intermediary products (eg sherry) and sparkling wine
2 litres of still wine
50 grams of perfume
0.25 litres of eau de toilette

The value limit for goods is 175 euros

Travellers under 17 years of age are not entitled to the tobacco and alcohol allowances.

NO
Drugs, firearms, ammunition, offensive weapons, obscene material, unlicensed animals.

CONSULATES

UK
☎ 965 21 61 90

Germany
☎ 965 21 70 60

USA
☎ 963 51 69 73

Netherlands
☎ 965 21 21 75

TOURIST OFFICES

Tourist Information Telephone Service
☎ 901 300 600

Tourist Information Offices
● Alicante (Alacant)
Rambla Méndez Núñez 23
Alicante 03002
☎ 965 20 00 00;
www.costablanca.org

● Benidorm
Plaza de Reyes de España
Benidorm 03500
☎ 966 81 54 63;
www.benidorm.org

● Dénia
Plaza Oculista Buigues 9
Dénia 03700
☎ 966 42 23 67; www.denia.net

● Elche (Elx)
Parque Municipal
Paseo de la Estación
Elche 03203
☎ 965 45 27 47

● Murcia
Plaza del Romea 4
☎ 902 10 10 70;
www.murciaturistica.es

● Orihuela
Palacio Rubalcava
Calle Francisco Diez 25
Orihuela 0330
☎ 965 30 27 47;
www.aytoorihuela.com

Other offices include: Altea, Águilas, Benissa, Calpe (Calp), Cartagena, Gandía, Jávea (Xàbia), Mazarrón, Santa Pola, Torrevieja, Villajoyosa (La Vila Joiosa) and Játiva (Xàtiva).

NATIONAL HOLIDAYS

J	F	M	A	M	J	J	A	S	O	N	D
2		(2)	(2)	1			1		1	1	2

1 Jan	New Year's Day
6 Jan	Epiphany
Mar/Apr	Good Friday, Easter Monday
1 May	Labour Day
15 Aug	Assumption of the Virgin
12 Oct	National Day
1 Nov	All Saints' Day
6 Dec	Constitution Day
25 Dec	Christmas Day

Many shops and offices close for longer periods around Christmas and Easter, as well as for the festivals of Corpus Christi in May/June and the local holiday of the *comunidad valenciano* on 9 October.

OPENING HOURS

○ Shops	● Post Offices
● Offices	● Museums/Monuments
● Banks	● Pharmacies

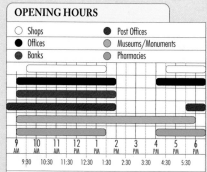

9 AM	10 AM	11 AM	12 PM	1 PM	2 PM	3 PM	4 PM	5 PM	6 PM
9:30	10:30	11:30	12:30	1:30	2:30	3:30	4:30	5:30	

Large department stores, as well as supermarkets and shops in tourist resorts, may open outside these times, especially in summer. In general, pharmacies, banks and shops close on Saturday afternoon. Banks may stay open until 4:30PM Monday to Thursday, October to May, but close Saturday, June to September. At least one chemist remains on duty in each town outside normal hours and at night. The opening times of museums is just a rough guide; some are open longer hours in summer than winter. Some museums close at weekends or another day in the week.

ELECTRICITY

The power supply on the Costa Blanca is: 220–225 volts.

Sockets accept two-round-pin-style plugs, so an adaptor is needed for most non-Continental appliances and a transformer for appliances operating on 110–120 volts.

TIPS/GRATUITIES

Yes ✓	No ✕	
Restaurants (if service not included)	✓	5%–10%
Cafés/bars (if service not included)	✓	change
Tour guides	✓	€1–2
Hairdressers	✓	change
Taxis	✓	5%
Chambermaids	✓	€1–2
Porters	✓	€1–2
Theatre/cinema usherettes	✓	change
Cloakroom attendants	✓	change
Toilets	✕	

WHEN YOU ARE THERE

PUBLIC TRANSPORT

Trains
The Costa Blanca is served by two railway systems. One links the main towns and runs to Madrid; the other is a scenic narrow-gauge line along the coast from Alicante to Dénia. The main RENFE (the Spanish railway network) lines link Cartagena, Alicante and Valencia, Alicante and Madrid, and Cartagena with Murcia (☎ 965 92 02 02; for English-language bookings ☎ 902 24 02 02; www.renfe.es). The Costa Blanca Express, run by FGV, leaves Alicante hourly from its own station and runs along the coast, stopping at virtually every station. Trains go as far as Benidorm, with about half completing the 2 hour 15 minute journey to Dénia (information and reservations ☎ 966 80 31 03).

Costa Blanca Buses
Alicante's bus station (☎ 965 20 07 00) is located on the Calle Portugal, from where buses leave for all over the province and further afield. There are several different companies serving the area. Their buses run hourly along the coast and link the province's towns. Tickets, with numbered seats, are bought in advance, and tourist information offices can provide details. In Murcia buses run from the bus station on Calle Sierra Nevada (☎ 968 29 22 11).

Boat Trips
Tabarca (► 48) is the main island of the cluster lying off the coast to the south of Alicante. Excursion ferries run from Alicante, Santa Pola and Torrevieja from April to November, giving a day on the island to explore and swim (information: Kon Tiki Alicante ☎ 965 21 63 96; Barco Santa Pola a Tabarca ☎ 965 41 11 13; Cruceros Tabardo ☎ 966 70 21 22).

Urban Transport
Local buses serve the main towns. Timetables and maps are available at local tourist information offices.

CAR RENTAL

The leading international car rental companies have offices at Alicante airport and you can book a car in advance (essential in peak periods) either direct or through a travel agent. There are also car hire companies in most of the main towns and resorts.

TAXIS

Hired at ranks (indicated by a blue square with a 'T'), on the street (by flagging down those with a green light/*libre* sign), or at hotels. They are good value, but may legally only carry four people. Check the approximate fare before setting out. A tariff list is displayed at taxi ranks.

CONCESSIONS

Students Holders of an International Student Identity Card can obtain some concessions on travel, entrance fees etc, but the major package-holiday resorts are not really geared up for students, being more suited for families and senior citizens. Package tours and camping offer excellent value and there are hostels and inexpensive hotels in the main towns for the more inquisitive traveller.
Senior Citizens The Costa Blanca is an excellent destination for older travellers, especially in winter when the resorts are quieter, prices more reasonable and hotels offer very economical long-stay rates. The best deals are available through tour operators who specialise in holidays for senior citizens.

DRIVING

Speed limit on motorways (*autopistas*): **120kph**

Speed limit on dual carriageways: **100kph**; on country roads: **90kph**

Speed limit on urban roads: **50kph**; in residential areas: **20kph**

Must be worn in front seats at all times and in rear seats where fitted.

Random breath-testing. Never drive under the influence of alcohol.

Lead-free petrol (*gasolina*) is available in two grades: Super Plus (98 octane), Super (96 octane). Diesel (*gasoleo* or *gasoil*) is also sold, although this is gradually being phased out. Petrol stations are normally open 6AM–10PM, though larger ones (often self-service) are open 24 hours. Most take credit cards. There are few petrol stations in the remote inland areas and they may not carry the full range of fuels.

If you break down driving your own car and are a member of an AIT-affiliated motoring club, you can call the Real Automóvil Club de España (☎ 915 93 33 33). If the car is hired, follow the instructions given in the documentation. Most of the international rental firms provide a rescue service.
Drivers must carry two warning triangles.

PHOTOGRAPHY

What to photograph: beaches, mountains, country villages, attractive harbours, markets, vineyards and olive and fruit groves.
When to photograph: the Spanish summer sun can be powerful at the height of the day, making photos taken at this time appear 'flat'. It is best to photograph in the early morning or evening.
Where to buy film: film and camera batteries are readily available from tourist shops and *droguerías*.

PERSONAL SAFETY

The national police force, the Policía Nacional, keeps law and order in urban areas. If you need a police station ask for *la comisaría*.

To help prevent crime:

- Do not carry more cash than you need
- Do not leave valuables unattended on the beach or at the poolside
- Beware of pickpockets in markets, tourist sights or crowded places
- Avoid walking alone in dark alleys at night

Emergency Telephone Number:
☎ **112**
from any call box

TELEPHONES

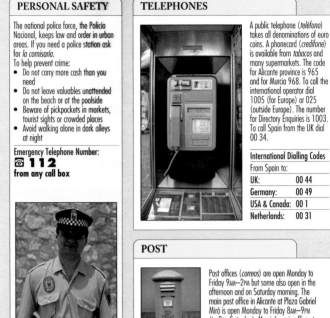

A public telephone (*teléfono*) takes all denominations of euro coins. A phonecard (*credifone*) is available from *tabacos* and many supermarkets. The code for Alicante province is 965 and for Murcia 968. To call the international operator dial 1005 (for Europe) or 025 (outside Europe). The number for Directory Enquiries is 1003. To call Spain from the UK dial 00 34.

International Dialling Codes	
From Spain to:	
UK:	00 44
Germany:	00 49
USA & Canada:	00 1
Netherlands:	00 31

POST

Post offices (*correos*) are open Monday to Friday 9AM–2PM but some also open in the afternoon and on Saturday morning. The main post office in Alicante at Plaza Gabriel Miró is open Monday to Friday 8AM–9PM (to 2PM Saturday). Murcia's main office at Plaza de Ceballos is open Monday to Friday 9AM–2PM, 5–8PM (to 2PM Saturday). Stamps may also be bought in *estancos* (tabacconists). Post boxes are yellow.

HEALTH

Insurance
Nationals of EU and certain other countries can get medical treatment in Spain with the relevant documentation (form E111 for Britons), although private medical insurance is still advised and is essential for all other visitors.

Dental Services
Dental treatment is not usually available free of charge as all dentists practise privately. A list of *dentistas* can be found in the yellow pages of the telephone directory. Dental treatment should be covered by private medical insurance.

Sun Advice
The sunniest (and hottest) months are July and August with an average of 11 hours sun a day and daytime temperatures that can reach 32°C. Particularly during these months you should avoid the midday sun and use a strong sunblock.

Pharmacies
Prescription and non-prescription drugs and medicines are available from pharmacies (*farmacias*), distinguished by a large green cross. Spanish pharmacists are highly trained and can dispense many drugs that would be available only on prescription in other countries.

Safe Water
Tap water is generally safe though it can be heavily chlorinated. Mineral water is cheap to buy and is sold as *con gaz* (carbonated) and *sin gaz* (still). Drink plenty of water during hot weather.

LANGUAGE

The language that you hear on the streets in the towns and villages of Alicante is likely to be either Castilian (Spanish proper) or Valencian, a written and spoken language closely related to Catalan. Valencian has been on equal footing with Spanish in the region of Valencia since 1982. Valencian thrives in large pockets throughout Alicante province but Spanish is widely spoken, particularly in the major tourist centres. Street signs, maps and newspapers are not yet consistently bilingual and for the visitor, Spanish still dominates in those places where English is not spoken. Murcia has always been Spanish-speaking.

hotel	hotel	bath	baño
breakfast	desayuno	shower	ducha
single room	habitación individual	toilet	lavabo
double room	habitación doble	balcony	balcón
one person	una persona	key	llave
one night	una noche	lift	ascensor
reservation	reservación	sea view	vista al mar
chambermaid	camarera		

bank	banco	bank card	tarjeta del banco
exchange office	oficina de cambio	traveller's cheque	cheque de viajero
post office	correos	credit card	tarjeta de crédito
coin	moneda	change money	cambiar dinero
money	dinero	cashier	cajero
cheque	cheque	foreign currency	moneda extranjera

café	cafè	starter	primer plato
pub/bar	bar	main course	plato principal
breakfast	desayuno	dessert	postre
lunch	almuerzo	bill	cuenta
dinner	cena	beer	cerveza
table	mesa	wine	vino
waiter	camarero	water	agua
waitress	camarera	coffee	café

aeroplane	avión	ticket	billete
airport	aeropuerto	single ticket	billete de ida
train	tren	return ticket	billete de ida y vuelta
bus	autobús	seat	asiento
station	estación de autobúses	car	coche
boat	barca	petrol	gasolina
port	puerto	where is...?	¿dónde está....?

yes	sí	excuse me	perdóneme
no	no	you're welcome	de nada
please	por favor	do you speak English?	¿habló ingles?
thank you	gracias	how much?	¿cuánto?
welcome	bienvenido	open	abierto
hello	hola	closed	cerrado
goodbye	adiós	today	hoy
good morning	buenos días	tomorrow	mañana
good afternoon	buenas tardes	help!	ayuda!
goodnight	buenas noches		

REMEMBER

- Remember to contact the airport or your tour company representative on the day before leaving to ensure the flight details are unchanged.

Index

TwinPack
Costa Blanca

Written by Sally Roy
Updated by Josephine Quintero
Revision management by Apostrophe S Limited

A CIP catalogue record for this book is available from the British Library.

ISBN-10: 0 7495 4335-3
ISBN-13: 978 0 7495 4335 8

Published by AA Publishing (a trading name of Automobile Association Developments Limited, whose registered office is Southwood East, Apollo Rise, Farnborough, Hampshire, GU14 0JW. Registered number 1878835).

© **AUTOMOBILE ASSOCIATION DEVELOPMENTS LIMITED 2003, 2005**
First published 2003.
Revised second edition 2005

Colour separation by Keenes, Andover
Printed and bound by Times Publishing Limited, Malaysia

ACKNOWLEDGEMENTS
The Automobile Association wishes to thank the following libraries and photographers for their assistance with the preparation of this book.

A1 PIX Ltd, London 47b; ANDALUCIA SLIDE LIBRARY/MICHELLE CHAPLOW front cover (c) woman; ANDALUCIA SLIDE LIBRARY/J.D. DALLET 48t, 48b.

The remaining photographs are held in the Association's own photo library (AA World Travel Library, 01256 491588) and were taken by the following photographers:
MICHELLE CHAPLOW front cover (b) pottery, (e) clock tower, (g) statue, (h) wine bottle, (i) mussels, bottom buildings, Back cover t (Alicante), ct (taxi), cb (restaurant), b (promenade), 5t, 6, 7, 8, 9, 12t, 12c, 12b, 13t, 14, 17, 18, 19, 20, 21t, 21b, 23, 24, 25t, 25b, 26t, 26b, 27, 28t, 28b, 29t, 29b, 31t, 31b, 32t, 32b, 34t, 34b, 35t, 35b, 36t, 36b, 37t, 37b, 38t, 38b, 39t, 39b, 40t, 40b, 41, 42t, 42b, 43, 45t, 45c, 45b, 46t, 46b, 49t, 50, 52t, 52b, 53t, 53b, 54, 55, 56, 57, 58t, 58b, 60t, 60b, 61t, 84, 85t, 85b, 90t, 90c, 90b; JERRY EDMANSON 15, 16, 30, 33t, 33b, 44, 47t, 49b; MAX JOURDAN front cover (f) bullfighter; ALEX KOUPRIANOFF front cover (a) oranges; KEN PATERSON 13b; JAMES TIMS 1, 61b; WYN VOYSEY 5b; PHIL WOOD front cover (d) palm tree.

A02011
Fold out map © Mairs Geographischer Verlag / Falk Verlag, 73751 Ostfildern
Cover maps © Geonext–Instituto Geografico De Agostini S.p.A., Novara

TITLES IN THE TWINPACK SERIES